Schools Reimagined

Schools Reimagined

Unifying the Science of Learning With the Art of Teaching

Jacqueline Grennon Brooks
Martin G. Brooks

Foreword by Michael Fullan

TEACHERS COLLEGE PRESS

TEACHERS COLLEGE | COLUMBIA UNIVERSITY
NEW YORK AND LONDON

Published by Teachers College Press,® 1234 Amsterdam Avenue, New York, NY 10027

Copyright © 2021 by Teachers College, Columbia University

Cover design by adam b. bohannon

Library of Congress Cataloging-in-Publication Data

Names: Brooks, Jacqueline Grennon, author. | Brooks, Martin G., author.
Title: Schools reimagined : unifying the science of learning with the art of teaching / Jacqueline Grennon Brooks, Martin G. Brooks ; foreword by Michael Fullan
Description: New York, NY : Teachers College Press, 2021. | Includes bibliographical references and index.
Identifiers: LCCN 2020046411 (print) | LCCN 2020046412 (ebook) | ISBN 9780807764961 (paperback) | ISBN 9780807764978 (hardcover) | ISBN 9780807779378 (ebook)
Subjects: LCSH: Constructivism (Education) | Educational change.
Classification: LCC LB1590.3 .B754 2021 (print) | LCC LB1590.3 (ebook) | DDC 370.15/2—dc23
LC record available at https://lccn.loc.gov/2020046411
LC ebook record available at https://lccn.loc.gov/2020046412

ISBN 978-0-8077-6496-1 (paper)
ISBN 978-0-8077-6497-8 (hardcover)
ISBN 978-0-8077-7937-8 (ebook)

Printed on acid-free paper
Manufactured in the United States of America

Contents

PART II: GUIDING PRINCIPLES

Foreword

There has been a great deal written about constructivism over the decades. Much has come and gone; little seems to stick. Yet it lingers in what we do (and by contrast, what we don't do). You won't find a more comprehensive, insightful, and memorable account of constructivist learning than what is provided by Grennon Brooks and Brooks in this wonderful cumulative account of what great learning is and how we should establish and pursue it.

What I love about this book is that it is simultaneously simple and complex—what we call simplexity. The authors start with the premise that schooling should be a search for meaning in the complex society in which we live, where discrepancies, confusion, and conflict abound and where each student, individually and sometimes together, has to seek to understand their experiences and ideas. The search for meaning is the central idea of this book.

I appreciate the stance and pursuit of personal knowledge in a social context because of my own work with colleagues in "deep learning" based on a premise we derived in working with students that we call "Engage the World Change the World" (Fullan, Quinn, & McEachen, 2018). In our work in ten countries, we found that students were increasingly disengaged as they moved up the grade levels, to the point that the majority ultimately found little direct purpose in schooling in relation to life. Our own alternative was to work with systems to enable students, teachers, and families to develop a set of global competencies that we called the 6Cs: character, citizenship, collaboration, communication, creativity, and critical thinking. And in turn to link these to a pedagogical model that contained four elements: inquiry-based pedagogy, partnerships, learning environment, and leveraging digital. Time and again I found that the chapters in *Schools Reimagined* resonated, chapter after chapter, with our own experiences.

After Part I on transforming schools and establishing "the Search for Meaning" as the foundation, there are five chapters in Part II that cover the essence of their model in terms of subject areas, big ideas, deeper reasoning, and a brilliant chapter on "responsibly assessing student learning." In Part II, Grennon Brooks and Brooks write comprehensively and succinctly as they show how learning designs can be applied, and how subjects (science, history, math, and more) can be best approached with an advanced pedagogical mindset. Part II contains the essence of their frame-work in action.

Part III, "Stepping Up and Speaking Out," contains two chapters that consolidate and frame the previous eight. In Chapter 9, "Shifting Norms and Structures," fundamental matters are established that frame the whole book. After all, this book is about radically transforming learning, and as such the authors take up: visioning and valuing; leadership; unity of pur-pose; establishing a culture of learning (comparing traditional and construc-tivist cultures); aligning curricula; collaborating with parents; differentiating rigor and equity, space and time, technology and distance learning; and an interesting reflection on "school as a concept."

The final chapter is called "Moving to the Next Level of Work." What I especially appreciated in this chapter, as a student of implementation, was a chart and section devoted to ten principles of "Quality Action." The list is comprehensive, clear, cohesive, and powerful! I tried to determine what I might disagree with and find wanting, but instead I found a list that was inspiring and complete. I am tempted to list all ten here, but will be content to name the first two and the tenth: Place the search for meaning at the center of educative practice; implement curricula that encourage the search for meaning through design challenges and big ideas; and confront and alter practices that interfere with social justice, equity, and access.

Schools Reimagined is a complete, succinct, and rich guide to new action—the kind of action that is badly needed as we develop a new system out of the ravages of COVID-19. A timely book indeed!

—Michael Fullan, professor emeritus, OISE/University of Toronto

Preface

This is a moment in time. The global health pandemic of 2020 has had a devastating impact across the world, in all nations, across racial and ethnic groups, affecting people regardless of their religion, political affiliation, gender identity, income, and job—although not equally. The long-term effects are unknown at this point but are likely to stretch into years, perhaps decades and, like the aftermath of other historical traumas, will undoubtedly forever change aspects of our daily lives.

Education has not been immune from the impacts of the pandemic. School buildings are opening and closing; state and federal aid to school districts have projected reductions; state and national examinations have been canceled; teachers have provided instruction remotely using technology in ways many had not used in the past or envisioned using in the future; administrators have redefined leadership, particularly pertaining to the remote collaboration with and supervision of staff; parents have become instructors in their children's learning and managers of emerging hybrid school and child care schedules; and we don't yet know the lasting lessons students are learning or the impact on their emotional well-being.

As we navigate these uncertain times, this uninvited experiment can create a new "normal" by abandoning what hasn't been working in education, resulting from policy dictates, and reclaiming the essence of learning and teaching, described by research and practice. We can stimulate individual and institutional changes based on what is known about how people learn. We can unify the science of learning with the art of teaching. To do so rests in acknowledging that students are naturally curious beings who search for meaning, whether at home or in school.

Openness to how we think about teaching and learning is essential. Part I of this book describes openness to the science of learning and what it tells us about the impact of constructivist education and openness to changes in instructional practice that align with this research. Part II focuses on the art of teaching and illustrates openness to new structures and ways of thinking about success; openness to greater teacher and student agency; and openness to schoolwork centered around big ideas, design theory, and authentic problems to solve. Part III portrays openness to shifts in school norms and structures that support the work described throughout the book, and openness to a set of ideas about how schools can move to their next level of work

In learning, authenticity matters. Context matters. Self-regulation matters. Self-correction of errors matters. And, in teaching, the skillful weaving of these factors into students' educational experiences matters. They matter in person, and they matter across cyberspace. Instead of filling in answers on worksheets on physical and chemical changes, imagine heading to the lab or the kitchen to study the changes in popcorn before and after popping. Children become scientists and journalists when they research their questions and document their findings. They become mathematicians and engineers when they select tools and measure quantities, linguists and anthropologists when they connect food to culture and heritage. In class, teachers circulate. In distance learning, teachers "teleport in" on their "rounds" and help students reflect on their work.

Imagine no worksheets on computing with mixed numbers and no frazzled adults at home trying to help children complete them. Instead, imagine students drawing floor plans of their rooms or houses or apartments, and finding out how many mixed numbers it entails, as well as how much measurement, spatial reasoning, decisionmaking, error, and new starts are involved. Instead of trying to remember and apply an algorithm that doesn't make sense, imagine inventing a system that works for their problem and then finding out for themselves if it works for other problems.

Imagine no more end-of-chapter test review questions and, instead, students and adults working together to design prototypes of needed items by hacking objects from around the house, using them to create something new. Remember the scene from the film *Apollo 13*, in which the engineers on the ground had to design a filter that would fit into the airflow openings on the spacecraft using only the materials available to the astronauts? Their final solution included ripping off the cover of an instruction manual and disassembling devices to use the parts in new ways. Today's children are both tomorrow's pioneers and the ones who will bring others safely home.

The essential purpose of schools is to empower children in becoming self-regulating, thoughtful citizens who can identify and solve significant problems and contribute to our healthy democracy. Whether planning a virtual classroom experience or a "real" one, we need learning options, contextualized in time and place, honoring students' unfolding curiosities, and fostered by caring, curious, judgment-free adults. Meaningful learning opportunities awaken the student in all of us.

When the pandemic struck, teachers across the nation rose to the occasion. They met remotely to develop plans with their administrators and colleagues. They created and/or identified new curricula for their students. They enacted these curricula with their students through the use of technology. They worked with students individually and in small groups and kept track of students' progress through these interactions. They determined ways to monitor and assess students' learning without administering tests. And they put all of this together in a matter of weeks. Their work was remarkable. That was then. This is now. Now, whether remotely or in-person, we are poised to imagine anew and reinvent.

As the pandemic has roiled our nation, another trauma has come into full view. The deaths of people of color, many at the hands of law enforcement, have cast a bright and long overdue light on the treatment of Black and Latinx people, both historically and today. Like the pandemic, schools are not immune from the impact of this soul-crushing plague. Schools, perhaps inadvertently, have been and remain guilty of institutional racism that is manifested systemically—in teacher and leader hiring practices, placement of students, student disciplinary procedures, selection of curriculum, assessment and grading of student work, classification protocols, student access to upper level courses, and numerous other areas. This situation cries out for a different form of openness—openness to self-examination, openness to hearing voices that have been muted in the past, openness to expanding opportunities for historically disenfranchised students and adults, and openness to changing systemic structures that privilege some students and adults while disadvantaging others.

Responsiveness to social justice is embedded in the educational approaches advocated throughout this book. Students of color, rather than being consigned to the dull busy work of test preparation activities as they too often are, must be offered opportunities to experience the richness and empowerment that voice and agency bring. To do otherwise is to knowingly continue racist practices in our schools.

The prequel to this book was first published over 25 years ago. We described how schools focused too often on essentially well-intended but very misguided instructional practices and metrics and made the case for a constructivist pedagogy in schools (Brooks & Brooks, 1993, 1999). Although efforts existed back then to educate students as thinkers, and we sought to nudge school curricula and practice further in that direction, national directives in the United States soon swept in, calling for the use of standards-based curriculum, data-driven instruction, and test scores as indicators of progress—an approach that has underpinned numerous failed reform efforts over the past 3 decades. In thinking about education for today and tomorrow, we can't continue repeating the errors of the past.

This book is intended for teachers, administrators, parents, and professors, offering images of next levels of work for schools, images that at times require shifts in the ways classrooms are organized and teacher roles are defined. Shifts are possible—the retooling of schools in response to the pandemic and the mobilization of action against racism have proved it. Now is the time to empower students as the self-regulating learners they are and can be if we are open to resetting perspectives and practices.

Acknowledgments

So many people have contributed to our thinking about education. We have spent our careers working with educators and students around the world who have opened their classrooms, their hearts, and their minds to us. We thank them for inspiring this book.

We thank Rob Altholz, Vivian Doremus, and Jennifer Gallagher for reading the first drafts of the manuscript and helping us find the right voice to tell the story we wanted to tell. Their feedback made a real difference.

Lunches with Elena Jurasaite-O'Keefe, Irene Plonczak, and Gloria Wilson became conversations about the structure and flow of the book. Dinners with Donna Migdol, Kathy Chapman, and Andrea Libresco became opportunities to discuss educational change and fine-tune the large issues and necessary details that make classrooms work. Cheryl Kurash has been an important teacher in mindfulness practice and a respected mentor in how to share it. Kathleen Reilly has been a consistently supportive thought partner from whom we have learned much.

Discussions over the years with Ann Cook, Galen Guberman, Joseph Hayward, Tom Heinegg, Michael McGill, Larry McGoldrick, David Quattrone, Marc Sharff, Sam Stewart, and the late Tom Sobol have enriched our thinking about school leadership and organizational change. Lauren Hubbard added texture to our thinking about students' civic engagement and environmental stewardship. Kathy Ernst has been a fellow constructivist traveler for many years and, most recently, our elementary school math guru. Cathy Bennett has been a standard for how to look closely; Lois Guberman, Maddie Stewart, and Pucci McGill guides for how to listen carefully; and Carol Van Duyn a model for how to open every classroom door with an open heart.

Walks around New York City with Lori Grennon, Margery Grennon, and Emily Brooks asking us probing and caring questions revealed the need for finer detail in order to make stories about classrooms more accessible. We are grateful for their insights.

Alexander Brooks and Morgan Hammel devoted hours on the back porch, around the fire pit, and at the kitchen table discussing the book's content and trying to help us craft a title that matched it. We hope we found it.

Teachers, school leaders, and district leaders with whom we have worked through the Tri-State Consortium, Hofstra University, and Long Island Explorium are deeply committed to enhancing the lives of the students entrusted to them. They continue to give us a cheerful glimpse into the future of education.

Finally, we wish to acknowledge the welcoming staff at Teachers College Press. Our editor, Sarah Biondello, and the TC Press team of Caritza Berlioz, Karl Nyberg, Nancy Power, Emily Freyer, and colleague Jitendra Kumar responded immediately to questions and guided us through the process of bringing the manuscript to press.

Schools Reimagined

MAKING THE CASE FOR CONSTRUCTIVIST SCHOOLS

Imagining Schools as . . .

Schools are always open, whether remotely or in person. They are worlds of limitless possibilities when we imagine them as such. In creating these schools, we open our thinking about teaching and learning, open new ways of understanding and assessing student performance, open discussions about how success is defined, open students' minds to the wonders of the natural and human-made worlds in which they live, and open students' hearts to ethical engagement in those worlds.

Imagine schools as laboratories, studios, or incubators in which new meaning, knowledge, and understandings are constructed daily by students and teachers, each of whom comes to school with a multitude of prior experiences, an active mind, curiosity, and a desire to learn more about the world.

These schools invite engagement. They become learning platforms that highlight discrepancies and confusion and guide students through the cognitive processes involved in examining new ideas, resolving contradictions, and building enduring understandings. Students who puzzle through discrepancies and challenge their present understandings construct new knowledge.

A SIMPLE PROPOSITION

Schools are at their best when their practices are aligned with what research tells us about learning, a process that begins with recognizing and valuing a simple proposition—as human beings, we search for ways to help us understand our experiences, to make sense of the ideas, objects, phenomena, and people we encounter each day. We seek to know. It is how humans are wired: To do so is simply human nature.

Our life experiences as thinking beings lead us to conclude that some people are generous of spirit and open while other people are closed and selfish; that two-party political systems either work well or don't; that squares are special types of rectangles or rectangles are special types of squares; that clouds sometimes, but not always, bring rain; and that basketball players usually are taller than hockey players. These represent a tiny fraction of the innumerable understandings we construct through reflection on our interactions with people, objects, information, and ideas each day—some of which are impressionistic, or based on partial information, or based on information generated by a biased source, or based on understandings from multiple, vetted sources. Each of us makes sense of our world by integrating and synthesizing new experiences into what we have previously come to understand.

When we encounter something that doesn't quite make sense to us, we either interpret what we see to conform to our present set of rules for explaining and ordering our world (we try to squeeze a round idea into our square mental scheme) or we generate a new set of rules that better accounts for what we perceive to be occurring (we create a new mental scheme to accommodate both square and round ideas). Either way, our existing thinking and new perceptions are constantly engaged in a grand dance that confirms or reshapes our understandings.

Consider, for example, a young girl whose only experiences with water have been in a sink, bathtub, and swimming pool. She experiences water as calm, moving only in response to the movements she makes. Now think of this same child's first visit to an ocean beach. She experiences the waves swelling and crashing onto the shore, whitecaps appearing then suddenly vanishing, and the ocean itself rolling and pitching in a regular rhythm. It looks different from the water she sees at home. It has a different smell, and it sounds different, too. When some of the water seeps into her mouth, the taste is entirely different from her prior experiences with the taste of water. She encounters a completely discrepant experience, one that does not conform to her prior knowledge of water. In response, she must actively construct a different understanding of water to accommodate her new experiences or deny the new information in order to retain her original understanding.

This persistence or transformation in thinking occurs, according to the classic work by Piaget and Inhelder (1971), because knowledge comes neither from the subject nor the object, but from the unity of the two. In this instance, the interactions of the child with the water, and the child's reflections on those interactions are leading to structural changes in the way she thinks about water.

As human beings, we experience and reexperience various aspects of the world, such as the ocean beach, at different periods of development, and thus continue to construct new and deeper understandings at different levels of complexity. The young child in this example came to know that the taste of seawater is unpleasant, and that waves can knock her over. As she ages, she might understand that ocean water tastes salty and that tides are predictable. As a teenager, she might understand that water can have different salinities, riptides can be powerful and dangerous, and the ebb and flow of tides relate to the lunar cycle. At some point in her development, she might examine how salt solutions conduct electricity or how the power of the tides can be harnessed as a source of usable, sustainable energy. Each of these deeper understandings will result from increased complexity in her thinking. Each new construction will depend on her cognitive abilities to accommodate discrepant data and perceptions, her fund of experiences at the time—and, of course, her interests, too. But it all begins, and continues to expand, around her need to make sense of what she encounters at each phase of her life and her concomitant, ongoing construction of new knowledge that stems from her persistent search for meaning (Brooks & Brooks, 1993).

Schools either facilitate or impede this process. When teachers recollect their most compelling experiences from their own schooling, they invariably talk about specific teachers who invited them to embrace and access the world's richness, empowered them to ask their own questions and seek their own answers, simultaneously honored and challenged their conceptions, and offered them opportunities to understand the complexities and interrelatedness of authentic issues and events that emerged daily in their lives. They were encouraged to dig more deeply into the questions that were important to them, reflect on their own experiences, think critically about the topics embedded in those questions, and explore directions that were of personal interest. All of this mattered greatly to them, as evidenced by their evocative recollections. Many report that they became teachers themselves because of these compelling opportunities in their own education. Knowing that their thinking mattered to their teachers mattered to them.

IMPLICATIONS FOR SCHOOLING

Policymakers and school leaders across the nation are grappling with consequential issues relating to student learning, teacher competence, social justice, and school quality.

Now more than ever, the time is right for an approach to schooling grounded in a culture of decency. On a global front, we have entered an unprecedented era marked by extraordinary partisanship, questions about whether facts are facts, unregulated proliferation of social media, marginalization of science, worldwide conflicts centering on ideological and geopolitical differences, climate change, global health challenges, and persistent threats to social justice. Our planet is increasingly dependent on citizens who can navigate through conflicting sets of information and form reasoned judgments about the veracity and value of what they hear and see, who can listen with open minds and communicate with compassion, civility, and rationality. Horace Mann, renowned early advocate of public education, wrote that the purpose of education is to foster "honest dealers, conscientious jurors, true witnesses, incorruptible voters and magistrates, good parents, good neighbors, good members of society" (1848, p. 599). Those words resonate now more than ever before.

States throughout the nation are charged with offering school-aged children a free and appropriate education. "Appropriate" is an ambiguous word, but structuring schools around the fundamental human quest to construct meaning and operating within a robust version of learning is undeniably appropriate—and has always been. In today's world, these actions are not just appropriate, they are urgent.

Parents want schools that offer their children the intellectual tools needed to make sense of what they experience, schools that are responsive to their children's interests in challenging yet compassionate ways, and educators who teach their children with a balance of academic rigor and personal kindness. Policymakers and business leaders want schools that educate students to embrace civic responsibilities and meet new work environments with flexible skills. Students want schools that give them voice and choice and opportunities to find meaning in the curricula they are studying. These different desires are not competing—they are complimentary.

Every day, millions of children come to school ready to be inspired and challenged. They appear at classroom doors with intelligence, hope, curiosity, questions, and a great appetite for learning—even if some may not overtly show it. They come to school each day hoping for recognition—even if some may not overtly expect it. And, they come to school each day in search of understanding—even if some may not overtly articulate it. In response, schools can either be places that acknowledge and respond to these aspirations, or places that don't. In schools that respond, we see lively students and purposeful teachers working collaboratively.

Many school leaders have earnestly been trying to create these schools. They have spent a good deal of money and effort updating curricula and resources and providing professional learning opportunities under the assumption that if the curricula are strong, the resources are appropriate, and the teachers are skilled at managing and delivering instruction, students will learn. Strong curricula, adequate resources, and skilled teachers are indisputably necessary. But the type of strong curricula, and the type of skill, and how and when they intersect matter enormously.

Key questions for educators relate to the extent their schools value compliance over self-regulation, memorization over thinking, and coverage of curriculum over development of personal meaning. Compliance with rules, memorization of information, and coverage of curriculum are deeply rooted aspects of schooling, but for enduring learning to occur they must be balanced with student agency developed through social interaction, critical thinking tied to creative thinking, and the construction of meaningful ideas.

Schools and the classrooms within them are complex social settings that set the frame for learning. Many schools have found welcoming ways to introduce improvements—for example, lengthening periods to allow for student investigations, implementing more descriptive report cards, and reducing repetitive homework. These shifts are positive, but do not necessarily change the fundamental teaching–learning dynamic. It's time to shift to a next level of work. The world in which we live calls for bigger changes.

PARADIGM SHIFT

Constructivism is the pedagogical underpinning of this book, an approach to teaching that represents, for many schools, a major shift in curriculum, instruction, and assessment. Constructivist pedagogy is built on the premise that people naturally search for understanding and construct meaning through experiences and reflection on those experiences. Its tenets and history are described in Chapter 3.

In the 1970s and early 1980s, research conducted to discern patterns in students' thinking used a process novel to educational research at the time. The researchers were the teachers. They did not study predetermined practices. Instead, they studied their own students' thinking and behaviors, created instruction in real time and in response to their hypotheses about the learning that was occurring and the cognitive breakthroughs that were within reach. The studies were called constructivist teaching experiments (Steffe & Ulrich, 2014).

The palette of constructivist teaching experiments elevated the status of teachers and gave them voice in curricular and instructional decisions. However, this approach to teaching and research receded with the publication of *A Nation at Risk* (U.S. National Commission on Excellence in Education, 1983), which lambasted public schooling as not sufficiently rigorous and ushered in an era of testing and accountability, an overarching framework that continues today much to the detriment of students and teachers, learning and teaching.

Looking at learners through the constructivist lens requires shifts in thinking for many educators, students, and parents. On the classroom level, changing from a more traditional teaching approach to a constructivist approach means much more than appending new practices to already full repertoires. It requires the willing abandonment of familiar perspectives and practices and the adoption of new ones. These shifts ask much of teachers but return many benefits.

In *Letters From the Earth*, Mark Twain (1909/2010) explored the human condition from the perspective of an extraterrestrial hovering unseen above the planet, observing our behaviors, customs, institutions, and rituals. If Twain's alien were to return to Earth today, well over a century later, it would discover that schools may look a little different but functionally operate much the same. Teachers still disseminate information and students still consume it. Students still take tests, receive grades, sit in classrooms, learn siloed subjects, and are still tracked and sorted into perceived ability groups. Technological innovations have changed the look of schooling, but the roles and daily functioning of the student and teacher remain largely unchanged.

Today, a teacher of a probability lesson might click on an interactive whiteboard as students watch animated dice tumble while the software records combinations and ratios. Whether the dice are real or virtual and whether computations are recorded on a chalkboard or whiteboard, students are still consuming information more than constructing knowledge, despite a significant body of research documenting the value of contextualized instruction through which students construct mathematical knowledge by solving real problems (Ball & Forzani, 2010/2011; Ernst & Ryan, 2014; Fosnot & Dolk, 2001; Ma, 1999; Schifter, 2001).

Guided by this research, a teacher might consider offering opportunities for students to study probability in different contexts. For example, some students may select virtual dice or real dice for problem solving—but only when dice are appropriate for the nature of the problem being addressed. Other students in that same class may use data charts, polling figures, or other materials, as appropriate for the problems they are solving. A textbook, a pair of dice, a smart watch, a photo, a chart—it is not the materials but how learners use the materials that determines the potential learning value of the lesson. Contextualization is essential for educators across other subjects, as well. Engaging with these types of problems enhances the likelihood of students becoming constructors of knowledge for themselves, and contributors to the construction of knowledge by others, too.

In another example, students studying ancient civilizations coproduce a lesson with their teacher by using their personal devices to submit images in real time to an interactive whiteboard, images of waterwheels and aqueducts as part of a study of structures across cultures. When students become contributors of resources to lessons, lessons become multidirectional with the voices of many contributing to the pursuit of collective and individual meaning. Within these lessons, concepts relevant to the topic as well as the spiraling nature of the curriculum emerge naturally from students' academic pursuits. The students "own" the lesson because they've contributed ideas toward it. They are fully engaged in the work.

Reflection on pedagogy uncouples educators from practices that put learners in the limiting role of receivers of information and opens opportunities for learners to become more active constructors of their own knowledge and contributors to discourse. The key questions for both educators and students are always: Why is this important to know or do (relevance and context), how can I contribute to the learning (agency), and why now (timing)? Relevance, context, agency, and timing are four critical factors in learning.

INFORMATION OR KNOWLEDGE?

The early childhood constructivist math educator, Fosnot, states that learning is not necessarily discovering more, but interpreting through a different scheme or structure (1993). There is a neurological explanation for this interpretation as well. The medical school educator, Dennick, describes the brain's interpretive functioning thusly: "the brain naturally attempts to extract meaning from the world by interpreting experience through existing knowledge and then building and elaborating new knowledge in a process identical to hypothetico-deductive reasoning or the scientific method" (2016, para. 7).

If Piaget and Inhelder were alive today, they might quarrel with the notion of "extracting meaning," wanting to substitute "constructing meaning," adding that no meaning exists "out there": Meaning is only constructed within the individual's mind through interaction and reflection. The pioneering research of Piaget and Inhelder, and other researchers discussed in Chapter 3, in connection with the groundbreaking research on brain functioning from the neuroscientific community, creates a call for change too compelling for educators not to heed.

There's a crucial difference between constructing knowledge and memorizing information. Information refers to discrete facts or raw data. Knowledge is broader, influenced by experience, and refers to understandings of how facts and data relate to each other, and how those relationships link to other knowledge. Information can be received. Knowledge must be purposefully constructed. This is true across disciplines.

Shifting from seeing learning as a process of adding information to a process of reshaping knowledge requires transformations in both pedagogical perspectives and classroom practice for teachers. Sometimes newly introduced facts and information don't fit with the knowledge students have previously constructed. When this happens, students often push that discrepancy to the side and work instead to store newly presented information in their working memory. It's an effective short-term strategy for mimicking learning and passing tests, but it results in a missed opportunity—because uncovering discrepancies and persevering to resolve them are essential components of deep and enduring learning.

In teaching how to compute the area of a triangle, telling students to use the formula $A = \frac{1}{2}bh$ presents the formula as a stand-alone piece of information. Its usefulness and transferability are limited to targeted sets of directed prompts. In order for students to use the formula to solve novel and contextual problems, students need to construct knowledge about what the formula actually means. To a mathematician, the formula is a shorthand statement that the relationship of the area of a triangle to that of a rectangle with the same base and height is 1:2. To many students, however, the formula is a unit of information to be memorized and applied to a specific set of problems. The difference represents the distinction between knowledge that endures and information that may not.

When the relationships among the areas of geometric figures become part of students' mathematical thinking and spatial reasoning, generated from seeing and understanding patterns across multiple figures, they do not forget. It's not likely that many students will accurately generate all formulas themselves, but some formulas, such as the area of a triangle, are within striking distance if students are provided the necessary opportunity, time, and support. Deriving the constant Pi, π, is another example.

About 2,000 years ago, Archimedes derived π. In some schools today, 3rd-graders are experiencing a similar "aha" by measuring the trip around and the trip across various sized circles with pieces of string and strips of tape. Students determine for themselves that the trip around any circle (circumference) compared to the trip across the same circle (diameter), no matter how big the circle, is always "about 3." Their eyes widen, and they search for bigger and bigger circles to test what they have discovered. After doing this, and with other follow-up "derivations," they don't forget $C = 2\pi r$ or confuse it with $A = \pi r^2$.

Research on remedial math courses in college supports the need for conceptually driven instruction. Kirp (2017) reports that more than two-thirds of all community college students are required to take a remedial math course; only one-third pass, and only 15% of students who take a remedial course earn a certificate or degree on time. He reports that some school districts are taking note, and a few are reframing their courses from memorizing math to thinking about math. Although some of these schools report concerns about time, efficiency, and coverage of content, they recognize the "reinvention" of concepts as a necessary component of the construction of knowledge and find that, paradoxically, reinvention is the most efficient way to learn big ideas and essential concepts. They conclude that it is students' desires to understand problems and their quest for efficient ways to solve problems, not teachers' efficient delivery of the syllabus, that creates the cognitive pathway to learning. Mentally building concepts, as different from amassing information, is a central component of sustainable, transferable learning that is not forgotten after tests or by the end of summer vacation.

Through constructing knowledge, which is different from memorizing information, learning is internalized, or "owned," by the student. It is transferred, transformed, and applied in solving all types of problems. Like the computers designed by human brains, the human brain itself is iterative; that is, it engages in cycles that revisit ideas, each time bringing new information from the last visit. Through these active, iterative processes, we all build concepts and create meaning.

For students to construct understandings at advanced levels of study, they need a priori opportunities to construct simpler understandings of more fundamental ideas. Every student's journey is different, either slightly or significantly, and each is marked by the unique characteristics particular to that student's cognitive functioning, experiences, and dispositions. Reinventing the wheel, seen by some education traditionalists as wasting time, is essential in understanding how the wheel works. Constructivist teachers see their role as facilitating each student's unique journey. All students are capable of learning—it's a simple but powerful statement of belief that undergirds practice.

MEANINGFUL WORK

As students age through the grades and their classes become more content oriented, the most engaged student learning and the most passionate teaching often occur in extracurricular activities, such as theater, debate team, newspaper club, and sports, and in elective courses, such as gender studies and green engineering (Mehta & Fine, 2019a).

> As different as these spaces were, we found they shared some essential qualities. Instead of feeling like training grounds or holding pens, they felt like design studios or research laboratories: lively, productive places, where teachers and students engaged together in consequential work. (Mehta & Fine, 2019b, para. 8)

Consequential work is meaningful work. It inspires higher-quality work. Students actively designing solutions to challenges they see as important and accessing the resources they need motivates them to learn. A design studio approach to mainstream education is likely to facilitate student engagement. We have known this for many years. Consider that 30 years ago, Glasser wrote:

> I have talked at length to groups of high school students about [quality classrooms,] and most of them see quality in athletics, music, and drama, a few see it in advanced placement academics or shop classes, but almost none see it in regular classes. While they believe they are capable of doing quality work in class, all but a very few admit that they have never done it and have no plans to do it in the future. (1990/1998, p. 2)

Every classroom can be a studio or a laboratory or a conservatory or a greenhouse or a workshop or a think tank. Educators can transform all corners of a school, or any space, into a landscape of multiple, interconnected learning platforms. Constructivist pedagogy is a powerful catalyst for these transformations. It shifts responsibility for learning to the learner. In constructivist settings, students do a lot of "starting from scratch" with teachers directing students to resources matched to their inquiries. This shift frees up teachers to spend more time interacting with students on concept-building activities.

TRACKING WORTHY OUTCOMES

Change starts with identifying and documenting worthy outcomes.

With the expansion of the testing and accountability movement, many schools participated in the federal Reading First initiative that sought to optimize instruction for decoding in grades K–3 using standardized approaches. After several years of funding and research, the Institute for Education Sciences reported "statistically significant impacts on instructional time" (Gamse et al., 2008, p. 27) and reported gains in decoding scores for 1st-graders (p. 26). But the report concluded that there exists "no statistically significant impact on reading comprehension" (p. 58). Consider the cost of the trade-off: Children learn the mechanics of reading at an earlier age, and some test scores related to decoding increase as a result, but there is no increase in student comprehension. Over time, this approach results in many students losing the disposition to be readers as they mature (Teale et al., 2007). Asking children to decode before they are developmentally ready to understand what they are decoding is a problem with a long-range, continuing cost. It's the wrong work, and test scores are the wrong metric.

On the other hand, there are place-based, contextual approaches to inviting children into explorations of the sound and sense of letters and encouraging children to communicate in print (McKay & Teale, 2015). Interestingly, development of executive functioning skills has been found to be more predictive of literacy achievement than phonemic awareness (Blair & Razza, 2007; Shaul & Schwartz, 2014). This research points to the role that self-regulated and coregulated classroom problem solving can play in fostering long-term reading comprehension strategies. "The emerging science of learning underscores the importance of rethinking what is taught, how it is taught, and how learning is assessed" (National Research Council, 2005, p. 72). These are the worthy outcomes of unifying the science of learning with the art of teaching.

As university professors often attest, high school graduates who obtain honors diplomas and excel in advanced level courses frequently have difficulty connecting textbook information with interpretations they are asked to construct of the world around them (Jones et al., 2014). Many enter college or the world of work with limited ability to transfer or apply what they were taught, largely because they never really had the chance to actually construct knowledge: They simply memorized facts with limited understanding of how the facts link to each other or can be applied to novel situations. For many of these students, success in school had more to do with memorization and compliance than with exploration and construction.

No one disputes that active construction of knowledge requires facts and information. In order to learn, we have to be thinking about "something." But, facts and information by themselves are readily forgotten if they have no context and are not used to deepen understanding of "something" bigger.

Not surprisingly, research has shown that success in school is often even more fragile for immigrant students. In an unsettling study, Adair et al. (2017) report on the responses of over 200 superintendents, administrators, teachers, parents, and young children, revealing how caring, experienced educators withhold a range of sophisticated learning experiences in the belief that children from immigrant homes lack the vocabulary to effectively engage in assignments requiring complex thinking. This, of course, results in a significant academic disadvantage for these students. Even more disturbing is the finding that children in these classrooms hold beliefs that learning requires being still, obedient, and quiet. The authors contend that well-intended educators, trapped in deficit-oriented thinking, unknowingly preserve discriminatory practices rather than stopping them. Too often, children from immigrant families learn in classrooms with fewer growth-producing opportunities than their native-born peers. This inequitable practice has to change.

AT A CROSSROAD

It is time to do the right work. For decades educators have been pressured to do the wrong work and, in many instances, have done it well—but it is still the wrong work. We have been operating under a system that values student compliance, holds curriculum as sacrosanct, enshrines test scores as proxies for what students know and can do, and misuses student test scores as metrics for gauging teacher competence and school quality. None of this has budged the needle on student learning, and that's what this book is about—student learning and how we can promote a more robust version of it.

Wherever one stands on education, it is clear that we are at a crossroad. One road is familiar and is built on the venerated, long accepted but structurally weak foundation of curriculum coverage and test score improvement as proxies for the quality of education. The other road, less traveled, is more nuanced and not as recognizable because it embraces the intricacies of teaching and learning as fundamentally human endeavors much messier and more complex than moving sequentially through a series of facts. This road places student learning and the construction of meaning at the core of educational change. Though less familiar, this is the road that takes us where we need to go.

We already know where the familiar road takes us—winners and losers, passing and failing, advanced tracks and remedial tracks, college bound and career bound, compliant and defiant. These are externally created and imposed categories, judgments and labels that sustain inequities, rewarding some students and harming others. The road less traveled offers a different approach to schooling, one through which teachers recognize and honor the capability and agency of their students and gauge success by changes in the richness and texture of their thinking, their engagement with others, and their work.

EVERY CLASSROOM A JOURNEY

Journeys begin with a direction. Innovative educator Seymour Papert quotes neurophysiologist Warren McCulloch as saying: "Don't bite my finger, look where I am pointing" (1965, para. 14). When thinking about changing school structure, let's point to schools that intentionally support imaginative minds, schools that stretch the delta of learning, schools that provide students some say in how they learn, schools that routinely gather multiple forms of evidence to calibrate and advance student learning, and schools in which every classroom is a journey.

Constructivist pedagogy democratizes schools. Rather than viewing students who have difficulty understanding or engaging with curricula as "slow" or "disenfranchised" or offering accolades to students viewed as "gifted" or "highly motivated," imagine schools that use judgment-free approaches and adapt curricula to students' present understandings. Imagine schools that endorse the notion that we are each in control of our own learning and we each construct our own individual understandings of the world. Imagine schools that embrace the reality that educators can guarantee opportunities, but not outcomes.

A transformative shift for many teachers is accepting that education is invitational—teachers can invite students to learn but can't mandate it. Learning is the province of the learner. Elmore writes:

> A truism of education is "I can teach you but I cannot 'learn' you," a phrase that is meant to convey the importance of the learner's active consent in the instructional process. Teachers require from learners their participation as active agents in order for learning to take place. (2005, p. 278)

See Figure 1.1 for a note that Adele sent to her younger cousin, along with a packet of her school spelling lists. Adele is "gifting" her cousin words she thinks he may need as he begins kindergarten, replete with her misspellings—and also her exceptional generosity of spirit.

Whether or not to accept Adele's generous invitation is her cousin's choice, which is a wonderful metaphor for how all students learn—it is their decision. Teachers who invite students into explorations with their own open minds and hearts and blend their individual talents with their understandings of how students learn maximize the likelihood of students saying yes to the invitation.

Figure 1.1. Adele's Note

> Dear william,
>
> Theis are words that you mightt nead in the Futer for spelling. thay ustow Be myn But I don ot nead them eny more
>
> Good luck.

PART I: MAKING THE CASE FOR CONSTRUCTIVIST SCHOOLS

Chapter 1 Imagining Schools as . . .	Schools moving to their next level of work open up thinking about teaching and learning, open new ways of understanding student performance, open discussions about how success is defined, open students' minds to the wonders of the worlds in which they live, and open students' hearts to ethical engagement in those worlds.
Chapter 2 Transforming Schools From the Inside Out	
Chapter 3 Searching for Meaning	

Transforming Schools From the Inside Out

If we accept that learning is controlled by the learner, then we must accept that teaching is controlled by the teacher. In this chapter, we look at classrooms from preschool through college with teachers who are transforming how they teach a topic that is also undergoing its own significant transformation: the dynamic Earth. This curriculum is taught at all levels and is of enormous importance as the Earth's climate undergoes continuous and currently dramatic change. As the teachers of these classrooms transformed their individual practice, they also played a role in transforming their schools—from the inside out.

For different reasons, the teachers in these classrooms all made the decision to alter their work to enable students to assume greater responsibility for their own learning and dive more deeply into the content being studied.

PRESCHOOLERS TAKE A NATURE WALK

Young children naturally try to make sense of the exploding natural world around them: why leaves change colors, why the sky looks blue on some days and gray on others, why clouds bring rain, why one day is cold and the next is hot, and the innumerable other ideas that fuel their growing understandings. Lessons on the changing Earth in preschool take many forms. In this example, it is a walk outdoors, a common activity in preschool settings.

To live responsibly in our world, we must care about it first. To care about it, we must understand it. Richard Louv, a leader in the movement to connect children, families, and communities with the natural world, has been a key figure in place-based, nature-centered learning, also called experiential learning (Louv, 2008). A walk outside is a productive way to begin the process of connection, and how a teacher scaffolds the walk has a huge impact on what students learn. Let's examine two different walks—the first with Ms. Adisa as she previously conducted her classes, and the second also with Ms. Adisa after reconsidering how children learn.

Ms. Adisa historically lined up the children in twos and instructed those on the left to pick up leaves on the left of the path, and those on the right to pick up leaves on the right. Once back in the class, the children traced each leaf, then colored them in. In one instance, near Thanksgiving, 4-year-old Harry asked if he could use his leaves as feathers to make the plumes of a turkey. Ms. Adisa agreed it was a good idea. Many other children liked Harry's idea and also wanted to make turkey pictures, and it wasn't long until the magic markers were out and the whole class was drawing. At that point, Ms. Adisa pulled up turkey outline drawings on the interactive white-board and printed one for each child. Ten minutes later, children were coloring the turkey outlines and gluing on leaves as the fanned tail feathers. The students discussed their turkeys with smiles and pride and took them home to show their parents.

Ms. Adisa perceived this to be a successful lesson. Her preschoolers were engaged and happy and created a product they liked, but Ms. Adisa also had a gnawing sense that her students could be learning more about their environment. She began to question the structure and purpose of the walks outside and the classroom activities that followed, wondering about the value of the nature study she was offering her students. By watching her students, she sensed the walks could be more than travel time and could lead to lessons that went beyond identifying colors and seasons. She began to understand how the walks might be part of the broader curriculum, op-portunities to learn about the life and Earth swirling around. Ms. Adisa's internal questions moved her to her next level of work.

She now takes her preschool students on different types of walks. On one of those days, Ms. Adisa prompted students to walk very slowly, look up, look down, look to the left and the right. "What do you hear? What do you not hear? What do you see? What do you not see?" She asked Abriana, who had lingered near a puddle, whether she could see different types of mud. Other children within earshot added to the mud conversation. (Yes, there are different types, and these 4-year-olds knew them all, and loved them, except for Tad, who didn't like any of them!) Another group lifted some rocks and spotted earthworms. Ms. Adisa asked if some of the earth-worms were moving faster or slower than others. (Yes.) She asked the bird-watchers if the birds they were spying seemed to like higher or lower tree branches. (It seemed they like high branches for singing, low ones for for-aging.) Ms. Adisa was inviting students to search for patterns. Emeka was bent down for a while looking at a small gray rock with an orange streak. Ms. Adisa offered to take a picture of her fascination, and said to Emeka, "Maybe we can find out more about that orange streak when we get back." Ms. Adisa was modeling how scientists approach their work.

Ms. Adisa also carried field guides in her pocket in case the children asked about a particular plant, rock, or animal that intrigued them—on this particular walk, none did. Back in the classroom, Ms. Adisa printed out photographs she took of features of the nearby natural environment, quietly placed them on tables around the room and asked the students specific questions about them, encouraging them to crystallize what they knew and speculate about what they didn't know. The students had many new thoughts and questions and asked if they were going on another walk the next day.

These two classes took two very different walks. Ms. Adisa's initial walks were for the purpose of collecting leaves for a separate activity. Back in the class, all students were engaged in the same task. When all the students ended up with the same work product, Ms. Adisa wondered if the children were stretching their own unique reasoning and artistry. That wondering brought Ms. Adisa to her new practice.

Ms. Adisa previously held a more traditional pedagogy that guided her in executing curricular plans with care and commitment but also limited learning opportunities for critical and creative thinking that might be fostered outside of those plans. Fueled by her broadened thinking, she now invites students into attentive study of their place and space. Many urban dwellers don't consider a walk on the sidewalk to be a nature walk, largely because they don't consider themselves out in nature. Ms. Adisa always did, and now even more so. She realizes that her urban students are in their natural environment, their nature, and she helps them see and hear the clouds, wind, birds, insects, trees, bushes, plants, and yes, weeds, too! In accord with Louv's research (2012), she understands that her students need to learn to live *within* nature, not merely learn *about* nature. She listens to and watches students in order to determine next teaching steps. She isn't sure what her students will find on any walk, what questions their discoveries will generate, or how they will react to their observations back in the classroom. But what she does know is that something unanticipated will likely be discovered, and that each discovery will likely lead to teachable moments. She routinely reviews the syllabus each week, makes daily plans, but knows that to offer the richest learning opportunities, she must tweak the daily curriculum to respond to emergent interactions with children.

Ms. Adisa is a constructivist teacher: Her students are building individual and collective understandings of their worlds, and she is responding to their growing understandings as learners. Of note is her current engagement in a program at a local university, a program focused on the biodiversity of local communities. Ms. Adisa wants to build a greater understanding of how to weave the environment into her daily work with students, and her skillfulness in weaving requires more content knowledge.

Ms. Adisa's desire to learn more about the science of nature has led her to wanting to know more about the science of learning. She is researching the impact of spending meaningful time outdoors, and its relationship to fostering early childhood academic success. Some small studies report that paying attention to bird calls and listening for other natural sounds may prepare children for recognizing basic word sounds (Martinelli, 2019). Ms. Adisa wants to know more. She is a midcareer teacher who is independently pursuing her own nature studies and new classroom approaches. She is transforming as an educator.

Next we meet a more senior educator who is a member of an informal study group in his school.

ELEMENTARY SCHOOL STUDENTS SIMULATE AN OIL SPILL CLEANUP

In today's schools, most teachers, regardless of pedagogy, use the Next Generation Science Standards (NGSS Lead States, 2013) or their states' equivalent to teach about the changing Earth. Let's meet Mr. Tan, a 5th-grade teacher addressing the grades 3–5 "Earth and Human Activity" strand:

Obtain and combine information about ways individual communities use science ideas to protect the Earth's resources and environment.

Over many years, Mr. Tan has selected National Science Teachers Association (NSTA) materials for his classroom. For this topic, he uses a lab-based, multiday, literature-inclusive simulation, *Simulating an Oil Spill to Understand Environmental Impact* (NSTA Press Picture Perfect Science Teaching Channel, 2019), and has found it effective in engaging students in exploring how communities can clean up noxious, harmful pollution. Today, Mr. Tan still uses the same resources but conducts the lesson differently than he once did.

Mr. Tan previously opened the lesson by reading the suggested picture book *Prince William* (Rand, 1994) and then sharing on the interactive whiteboard a set of slides he put together depicting actual oil spills that occurred in the past, and the varying processes of cleanup. He asked his students questions about the impact of oil spills and collated their responses into a list he posted on the wall. He created his own student worksheet for the lab so that all the students would proceed in the same manner and sequence. Mr. Tan distributed the materials (coffee filters, pipettes, cotton balls, etc.) as he paced the lesson. He instructed students on the proper materials to use, shared tips on how to use the materials most efficiently, and explained how to track findings on the worksheet. The students followed his directions carefully. All of their engineered creations, mostly identical, successfully absorbed much of the oil. Mr. Tan's measure of success was cleaner water and completed, accurate worksheets. However, over time, something began to trouble Mr. Tan, who came to see the lesson as more about following directions on how to do the work than about the work itself. He decided to rethink his approach.

Now, Mr. Tan prepares for the lesson by getting a few books from the school library, bookmarking websites on the class whiteboard, and collecting pictures of prior oil spills. He prepares the lab supplies and sets them up, labeled and categorized, on a table rather than distributing them to the students. He prepares the ocean oil spills for each pair of students and has them ready on their tables when they enter the classroom. He also has prepared backup ocean spills in reserve, just in case some students make irreversible errors and wish to begin anew. He opens the lesson by telling the students that while they were out of the room, terrible oil spills occurred in the model oceans on their tables and that he is hoping they all can design ways to clean them up. He ends with: "Start with what you think will work best and get to work. Use anything on the supply table that might be useful. Let me know if there is anything else you need."

In response to his introduction, Mr. Tan's students commonly look around and wonder how to begin. They often ask him how to proceed. Mr. Tan tells them to talk with each other and decide what approach to take, what materials to try first. After some hesitation, students begin their first trials. Mr. Tan circulates, taking note of each group's approach, and offering differentiated feedback on how they might proceed or how they may track their findings. With a few groups that finish up their first trial quickly, he sends them to the library to check out books related to the process they are using and the processes commonly used commercially in real spills—books he had spotted in his preparation but left on the shelf for students to find at a time that he thought would be the most meaningful to them. Some groups choose to conduct Internet searches. With some groups, Mr. Tan asks questions about sequencing of processes or purposes of techniques; with other groups, he poses questions about biological consequences (life cycle interruptions) or economic implications (decline of livelihoods from fishing). His specific questions depend on his sense of each group's needs and interests. But his general strategy is to ask questions that invite pattern seeking.

Mr. Tan still uses the same materials that he used in prior years, but there are significant process and outcome changes: His students now ask greater numbers of questions about content than about procedure; his students assume self-selected roles, with some emerging as leaders and initiators in one instance and managers and recorders in others; and different students are raising their hands with questions. Mr. Tan is discovering new capacities in his students. He sees more collaboration among classmates and more commitment to accomplishment. One of his students recently said, "I think more about my ideas than my grade."

Mr. Tan's new measure of success is the extent to which his students continue to talk about, reflect on, and process what they have done—their level of engagement in design processes, their documentation and communication of intent and processes, their analysis of what worked and didn't work, and the science concepts they build through their engineering activities.

It is important to note that when social distancing is required, the sharing of materials from a central source reverts to presorted materials at each student's desk and group work changes to individual work. When remote learning is in place, students prepare their own spills and gather their own material at home.

Mr. Tan's practices are now more aligned with constructivist pedagogy. In his prior classes, every student's oil cleanup was successful. Within his new approach, some students don't clean up the oil spill very well, and they often want to retry their experiments. They ask for more time and do so with greater self-agency than Mr. Tan had previously witnessed. Part of Mr. Tan's new definition of success includes the ability of his students to explain why "failure" occurred, and how new attempts might be structured.

Mr. Tan's transformation began when he joined a professional learning community in his school, a loosely coupled group of teachers intrigued by new ideas emerging from the neuroscience community. Reading about new ideas led Mr. Tan and his colleagues to "old" ideas—ideas like "Neurons that fire together wire together" (Hebb, 1949). Knowing more about the plasticity of the brain intrigued him and implied that his role as a teacher may be even more powerful than Mr. Tan thought as he began his career. This foray led him to other "old" ideas from the field of cognitive development, and his interactions with colleagues caused him to reflect on how he, himself, learned. This led him to appreciate the need for his students to invent and reinvent their knowledge, much as he was doing. He understood that student experimentation with their own ideas is a scholarly activity. Mr. Tan's transformation jump-started a reinvention of his own professional life, moved him to his next level of work—and also opened up new learning spaces for his students.

The next teacher is an early career professional in a master's program that is prompting her to reflect on her conceptions of success.

MIDDLE SCHOOLERS RESPOND TO A GLOBAL CHALLENGE

Ms. Goodwell and her classes are addressing the following middle school NGSS standard within the topic of the Dynamic Earth:

Construct an argument supported by evidence for how increases in human population and per-capita consumption of natural resources impact Earth's systems.

Last year, Ms. Goodwell used an Earth Science text from a well-regarded publisher. Ms. Goodwell assigned readings for homework. She reviewed the material in class, and then referred students to the textbook chapter review questions, allowing students to self-select into small groups to discuss answers. Two examples follow.

One of the review questions asks:

What is the ozone hole?
A. the region in which radiation is absorbed
B. the layer of the atmosphere
C. a depletion of ozone in the ozone layer
D. a type of Freon

Another review question asks:

What contributes to acid rain?
A. carbon dioxide and oxygen
B. sulfur dioxide and nitrogen dioxide
C. sulfur dioxide and carbon dioxide
D. nitrogen dioxide and oxygen

These questions, both appropriate to the content being studied, illustrate the type of thinking in which students had been engaging in these textbook-guided lessons. Ms. Goodwell incorporated some of the text's suggested activities into class lessons and supplemented the text with homework assignments using data charts on population growth from the organization *Our World in Data* (Roser & Ortiz-Ospina, 2017), and per-capita consumption charts from the National Oceanic and Atmospheric Administration (NOAA, 2017). Ms. Goodwell's students seemed to be learning the material, as demonstrated by their scores on end-of-chapter tests, and she was pleased with their performance.

This year, Ms. Goodwell, a provisionally licensed teacher in a master's program leading to professional certification, is using a new approach in the unit—not that she really wants to use this new approach, but completion of her master's thesis requires an action research project, and with encouragement from her professor, she has chosen this unit to study. Recently, she launched a lesson inspired by a selection from *People's Curriculum for the Earth* (Bigelow & Swinehart, 2014), a collection of articles written by authors, mostly classroom teachers, who share lesson ideas about dynamic Earth systems through use of simulations and primary data, incorporating stories and poems about real people and places and materials from public sources. All of the resources aim at connecting practices and phenomena to real-world issues, such as agricultural norms, consumer culture, fossil fuel use, and mining in indigenous people's communities, as they relate to changing Earth dynamics.

Ms. Goodwell selected "The Mystery of the Three Scary Numbers" (p. 185), an activity of deduction with separate clues about three numbers:

2 degrees Celsius (the warming level at which the planet's sustainability is threatened), 565 gigatons (an estimate of the CO2 that can be put into the atmosphere with a reasonable chance of keeping warming below the threatening 2 degrees Celsius mark), and 2,795 gigatons (the amount of CO2 in reserve ready to burn, much exceeding the 2 degree mark). Some cues are graphs, such as the often-cited graph tracking the carbon dioxide content in the atmosphere at the famed Mauna Loa Observatory, and some are research summaries of Congressional Budget Office studies on, for example, the relationship between personal wealth and human consumption that releases carbon dioxide.

As students interact with each other, consulting their textbook and online resources as needed, Ms. Goodwell carefully listens for the leading edges of students' thinking: Where are they in their understanding of the issues embedded in the lesson, and what do they need to know to continue progressing in the activity? This is challenging and sometimes mentally exhausting work, and Ms. Goodwell feels alternately excited about student engagement and overwhelmed by managing so many resources and ideas simultaneously—and also overwhelmed because she now is focusing on individual students, not the class as a whole.

To students discussing the Mauna Loa data, Ms. Goodwell suggests that they find out more about Charles David Keeling, reasoning that researching the person behind the establishment of the carbon dioxide study and the iconic figure for which the graph of the data is named (the Keeling Curve) would extend that group's inquiry. Ms. Goodwell directs a group discussing the environmental implications of coal exports to view a short video from NASA Earth Observatory (2017) that introduces variables not yet considered by them. She had initially planned to bring per-capita consumption into full view and revolve the lesson around her students' ability to amass appropriate evidence for a debate about this issue. However, she determined that a continued focus on developing better understandings of the carbon cycle was the more appropriate learning priority at that point.

In the past, Ms. Goodwell focused her teaching on the acquisition and potential application of information. Now, she directs her teaching toward fostering her students' creation of transferable knowledge. Previously, Ms. Goodwell intentionally invited students to work in groups, provided access to primary source materials, engaged them in discussions of complex issues, and assessed their learning using the textbook's questions. It is how she was taught, and it all made sense to her, but as Ms. Goodwell reflects on the past, she comments that although her former students were comfortable with her classes and studied important topics, she recognizes that she did not engage them in the full spectrum discourse and action she offers her students now—iterative opportunities to understand root causes of greenhouse gases, the role of predictive statistics from multiple domains, and the rights and responsibilities of collective human actions, with emphasis on how those issues relate to the Earth's sustainability.

Last year in Ms. Goodwell's class, climate change was a topic to be covered in the science syllabus. This year is different. The textbook is a resource, not the lesson framework. With a new pedagogy, Ms. Goodwell reports that her students have a better understanding of the carbon cycle and its integrated role in nature. More importantly, Ms. Goodwell and her students, together, began to better understand climate change as a global challenge in need of whole community responses that reach beyond individual change in consumption and behavior. Teacher and students are learning together. Ms. Goodwell's journey to her next level of work includes a transformation launched by her own graduate studies and fueled by her students' transformations as learners.

The high schoolers in the next featured classes are taught by two veteran teachers in two different schools within the same city. Through a professional learning opportunity, they decided to experiment with a constructivist approach to a unit that they have both been teaching for years.

HIGH SCHOOLERS BECOME STEWARDS OF WATER QUALITY

Ms. Dale and Ms. Chang teach in very different schools (one public, one private), and teach the unit of study, "The Interplay of Society and Environment," within different school structures—one within a yearlong academic course that is part of the general program, another in a 1-week elective course, during a semester interval, selected by students based on interest.

This year, both teachers are trying something new. Instead of presenting categories of issues to students with multiple examples, they are introducing a water quality dilemma and focusing lessons on one big idea, the complexities of managing society's competing economic, cultural, and political interests with stewardship of the environment. The teachers are tailoring their lessons to groups of students as issues emerge from student inquiry and research. Ms. Dale is teaching the unit through a multidisciplinary exploration of the competing water needs of diverse communities impacted by a river running through several adjacent regions. Ms. Chang is teaching the unit through a multidisciplinary exploration of how to enhance public appreciation of the need to conserve and better utilize the water of a harbor situated near a rapidly developing coastal town.

In previous years, both teachers structured the unit similarly, largely around textbook assignments and a culminating presentation. They scaffolded the unit by delineating requirements: For example, students needed five required bullet points for the oral presentations, citations from at least three vetted sources, three pieces of relevant information on each index card, and so on. The teachers reported that student questions mostly focused on compliance with instructions and procedures: "Am I doing this the right way?" The teachers had anticipated that preselected articles from historical and current sources would respond to students' questions but found instead that there were few content questions and instead most of the students' questions centered on whether their work was sufficient to earn the points associated with each step. Understanding the content became subordinate to earning a high grade.

This year, within their new approaches of working with students on water use scenarios, both teachers found that they were offering different types of scaffolding than they had originally planned to provide. Students' interests quickly began to drive their work, provoking different types of teacher engagement, which, in turn, required the teachers to adjust their notions about how to develop the lessons. The students became immersed in the challenges and asked content and conceptual questions of a higher order and on a more expansive plane than the teachers had experienced in the past.

Additionally, the teachers both identified five common takeaways from their interactions with their students, all centered around the compelling nature of the work in which they were engaged:

- Discussions with students became unique to each group's focus, and the teachers found themselves considering issues new to them and helping students find more detailed information than their original curricular plans anticipated.
- Students asked fewer questions about compliance with assignment format and requirements, and instead asked more questions about water flow and resource allocation.
- Fewer students asked if their answers were correct, and greater numbers of students commented on the complexity of policymaking, natural resource management, and conservation education—the big ideas of the lessons.
- Many more students continued to discuss their work outside of class time, in the hallways and lunchrooms, and in seats before classes began.
- Time allotted for end-of-unit assessment was reduced because observation of and interaction with students had already provided significant evidence of students' knowledge of the content. Performance assessments were organized to permit the students to educate their classmates as well as to evaluate their learning.

Ms. Dale and Ms. Chang learned the value of problem-based, big-idea curricula challenges. It's complex work, and it took them time to hone their new skills. For example, they initially established routines to elicit student voice, such as turn-and-talk opportunities, believing that these routines would enable students to demonstrate what they know and how they are thinking. However, because both teachers initially used this time to collect or return student papers and engage in other noninstructive tasks rather than listen to the conversations, they both quickly realized that they were losing the opportunity to ask students' clarifying questions and hear their viewpoints. Organizing procedures for seeking students' viewpoints requires careful listening. Ms. Dale and Ms. Chang reflected deeply on their practices and moved to their next levels of work through understanding that shifts in practice must accompany shifts in curricula in order to maximize student learning.

These two veteran teachers recognized that their new approach was more intellectually rewarding for their students, as well as for them. They discovered that big ideas are seen by students as engaging and relevant. It was a revelation for them that continues to benefit the students they teach.

Lastly, we present the story of an interdepartmental group of college professors who work together to change the Dynamic Earth Systems course by targeting their instruction on civic engagement and responsibility.

UNDERGRADUATES INCLUDE SOCIAL JUSTICE IN STUDIES OF THE CHANGING EARTH

In many university science departments, students study Earth Systems in separate lectures on tectonic plate drift, crust quakes, volcano eruptions, air pressure changes, storm formation, precipitation rates, and a sequence of other topics. Typically, a course midterm and final exam are used to monitor and assess student learning. This is a traditional structure, and within it, mostly through memorization, the acquisition of important information can and does occur.

But, does this approach maximize the likelihood that deep, enduring learning will occur? Research says, "no" (Smith & Colby, 2007; Zeiser et al., 2016). And, we suspect the recollections of readers who spent many years attending well-delivered lectures from scholars in the field also say "no." Engaged learners typically follow lectures as they unfold and note what is being said, but unless there is a relevant context or a problem to solve that engages them in using the information in a meaningful way, most students don't remember the information—which implies they didn't actually learn it.

College courses that cover important scientific information within pressing environmental issues provoke civic engagement, action, and responsibility related to potential solutions. One example is an interdisciplinary approach to investigating dynamic Earth systems—a case study of the Hawaiian Archipelago, a geographically isolated set of islands in the Pacific Ocean. This case study provides a context within which students examine the effect of human economic behavior on climate science, and the role of policy in balancing issues of nature, humanity, and social justice (Konan & Morgan, 2016). In this case study, professors of ocean and earth science, along with professors of economics and philosophy, work together to facilitate students' self-organized teams around a challenge that anchors the semester's research. Addressing this challenge also develops students' leadership competencies and heightens commitment to their own learning. Final representations of learning include a variety of student creations—speech, white paper, set of talking points, and debates, among others.

Within this structure, the science of changing Earth processes is studied in conjunction with habitats, governments, economics, and lifestyles, all of which are changing Earth processes while Earth processes are changing them. The professors found their next level of work by recognizing that students' enhanced content knowledge must be accompanied by deeper understanding of social justice issues embedded in the interconnectedness and complexity of the ever-changing natural, political, social, and economic worlds—and that context and authenticity matter greatly to their students.

TEACHERS TRANSFORM THEIR PRACTICE

The teachers described in this chapter illustrate that content alone is insufficient as a motivator for student learning: It must be combined with purpose, and that purpose must be seen as meaningful by learners. "Why" always matters. These teachers, reflecting on their own work, came to recognize and honor the basic human impulse to construct new understandings, and they opened possibilities for students by offering them voice and choice. They allowed students to connect what they were learning to bigger ideas.

These teachers placed in students' hands the exhilarating power to follow trails of interest, to make connections, to err, to reformulate ideas, and to reach unique, personally meaningful conclusions, conclusions that may be altered yet again when confronted with even newer information. They set the stage for students to generate their own rigor and shared with students the important message that the world is a complex place in which multiple perspectives exist and personal interpretations frame present understandings. They embraced the messiness of facilitating rather than the neatness of instructing, and acknowledged that learning and assessing learning are, at best, elusive endeavors with fuzzy lines, peaks and valleys, and stops and starts, and that trying to control everything their students think and learn is not just impossible, but counterproductive.

These teachers challenged their original assumptions about both teaching and learning, and found them inaccurate, partial, or limited. They felt the need to change and made adjustments in line with the science of learning, which is discussed next in Chapter 3. Their collective work offers visions of what is possible, and these possibilities can be pursued in all settings.

PART I: MAKING THE CASE FOR CONSTRUCTIVIST SCHOOLS	
Chapter 1 Imagining Schools as . . .	Schools moving to their next level of work open up thinking about teaching and learning, open new ways of understanding student performance, open discussions about how success is defined, open students' minds to the wonders of the worlds in which they live, and open students' hearts to ethical engagement in those worlds.
Chapter 2 Transforming Schools From the Inside Out	Teachers who transform their practice through reflection on assumptions, processes, and outcomes transform the schools in which they work.
Chapter 3 Searching for Meaning	

Searching for Meaning

It is human nature to seek meaning. On our way to work we encounter a traffic jam, and we seek to know why: an accident, road work, or just volume? We ask Siri or turn on a navigation app to understand what we can do to work our way around the problem. We get into school and are told a meeting has been called by the principal. We immediately seek out colleagues to see if they know why. We teach our first class of the day and discover that Ramona is absent. Why? During the first break, we go to the main office to find out about Ramona. And on and on.

Life is a constant search to understand. Many fields of study are co-alescing into a compelling view of human learning that argues strongly for a different approach to schooling. This chapter documents the research of scholars who have studied and are studying cognition, development, and psychology and connects it with neuroscientific research that adds explanatory support for the learning potential of constructivist classrooms. Their work explains the search for understanding and anchors this book.

MAKING SENSE OF THINGS

How do students, actually *all* of us, search for understanding? When confronted with new objects, we study them and decipher the purposes for which they can be used. When exposed to new ideas, we reflect on them, blend them with our preexisting understandings, and try to make sense of them. When meeting new people, we engage in ways that help us determine who they are and what they value. It is through these individual cognitive processes involving interactions with others, objects, ideas, or phenomena that we each construct the basic schemata and principles that frame and connect us to our worlds and everything in them.

It is no different for our students than it is for us. They're assigned to read a poem by Donne and want to know why. What is it about this poem that resonates with the teacher and separates it from the thousands of other poems she might have asked them to read? When a pebble is thrown into a body of water, floating objects move in toward the ripples, not away from them. This phenomenon seems counterintuitive, but the evidence is clear.

How is this explained? Is it really possible that the assassination of an arch-duke began World War I, which resulted in millions of deaths, or were there other, less well-known reasons—and if so, what were they?

We all have questions about our worlds, whether we pose them or not. This is true for every student in our schools, even pertaining to the most seemingly trivial aspects of schooling: Why are we being organized alpha-betically; why do we line up by height; why do we need permission to go to the bathroom; why do "periods" last 42 minutes; why are we given home-work; and many, many other questions relating to all aspects of their school life. And, of course, students have deeper questions pertaining to more com-plex issues they witness in their lives, questions such as: Why do some dis-eases affect certain people more than others; what's the difference between Black Lives Matter and Blue Lives Matter and All Lives Matter; and why is immigration such a source of contention across the world?

It is almost impossible for teachers to know what their students are thinking about and questioning. Capturing another person's understanding is, if anything, a nuanced enterprise. Unlike the recitation of memorized in-formation, the act of transforming ideas into more comprehensive ones of-ten transcends concise description. Teachers "see" neither the transformed concept nor the process of construction that preceded its transformation. What teachers do see are students' new behaviors or products or statements. They look not for what students can repeat, but what students can gener-ate, demonstrate, perform, and exhibit, and also their self-reflections on their own growth. These are school-based proxies for the meaning students make, along with listening carefully to what students say to teachers and classmates—and they say a lot.

People build cognitive structures through which they construct ideas, and, in turn, new ideas promote the development of new cognitive struc-tures (Piaget, 1977, 1985). When experiences and reflections on those experiences fit with current understandings of how our worlds work, all usually makes sense and we remain in cognitive equilibrium. Piaget called this process *assimilation*. When our experiences are in conflict with current thinking—when we perceive a discrepancy, or what we see isn't adding up, or new information doesn't jive with what we think we know—we feel cog-nitive *disequilibrium*, recognize the conflict, let go of previous understand-ings, and construct new ones. This process is called *accommodation*.

In the field of psychology, letting go of anger and other toxic emotions is seen as an important step in advancing one's emotional development. Similarly, letting go of old ideas and beliefs is an important step in advanc-ing one's cognitive development. It opens space for growth.

Lessons focused on the accumulation of information simply add more to the siloed piles students already have created for storing this information. Lessons focused on the making of meaning enable students to question and/or use what they have placed in those piles and, in so doing, help them to transform old ideas that no longer explain what they see and how they think into reformulated ideas that do.

OUR PERSONAL PANTHEON

We began contemplating the search for meaning and the construction of knowledge many moons ago, as young educators. Our lifelong inquiry into constructivist pedagogy had an unlikely beginning: a claim from a biophysicist that he had a biological explanation for Jean Piaget's stage theory of cognitive development (Epstein, 1978). The idea was intriguing and we wanted to know more. With colleagues from our school district, we attended a summer institute. From there we organized a professional learning program, Cognitive Levels Matching (Brooks et al., 1983), so that teachers in our district could learn more about cognitive development research, theories, and potential applications.

Although it turned out that Epstein was not able to prove his hypothesis—that growth spurts in brain circumference correlated with Piaget's stages—for us his work was a spark. As we began to learn more about Piaget's renowned stage theory, we began to understand that his stage theory of cognitive development was actually far less relevant to classroom instruction than his descriptions of the processes by which mental structures become more complex over time. We moved our attention to the interplay of Piaget's notions of assimilation, accommodation, and equilibration, convinced that a closer look into these processes would allow us to align classroom practice more closely with the natural unfolding of students' reasoning capacities.

Learning to Understand Piaget

Patricia Arlin (1975) became a valued mentor as we sought to better understand Piaget's pioneering methods of researching children's cognitive development (Piaget, 1955). Piaget's qualitative observations of the logic and reasoning of children's responses in problem-solving situations are the most noted feature of his "clinical method," capturing the outwardly observable indicators of children's thinking over time. Piaget posited that transformation of thinking results from the construction of increasingly complex cognitive structures, which he called schemata (Piaget, 1952). We were excited to know more about these inferred structures.

The work of Barry Wadsworth (1989) provided clarity: These *structures* allow people to engage in the *processes* of assimilation, accommodation, and equilibration, processes that describe how people adapt to and organize their environments. Wadsworth deepened our understanding of Piaget's work and prepared us for the detail and precision of Piaget's writings. Ed

Labinowicz (1980) offered many examples of problem-solving tasks suitable for use in schools, revealing how students interpret reality and seek balance between cognitive stability and cognitive change.

Marcia Linn (1983, 2006) applied Piaget's clinical interview methodology in multiple long-term studies, leading to what she later called "perspectives on knowledge integration," a view of conceptual change that includes understandings of how students build knowledge, structure it, and transform it (Clark & Linn, 2013). Working with colleagues, we used the deep listening procedures embedded in the clinical method when working with groups of students to better hear what they were thinking as they solved problems.

We met with Hans Furth and introduced young children to the carefully constructed activities that he and Harry Wachs (1975) designed to facilitate the development of logic. David Elkind became another significant mentor as we dug further into the complexities and challenges of teaching middle school students. He enhanced our understanding of adolescent thinking, particularly focusing our attention on how egocentrism increases during early adolescent years and what it means for teacher–student interaction (1978, 1981).

Eleanor Duckworth (1972, 2006) emerged as another teacher for us. She studied children's thinking in the physical sciences and wrote extensively about intellectual development emerging from experimentation. Her commitment to teaching practices that allow children to think freely and have "wonderful ideas" gave us the agency to transform our practices in ways that incorporated student voice. Her work applies to adults, as well, so we incorporated her ideas in many of our peer-led professional learning sessions. From Irving Sigel, we learned to look at teaching as a conceptual art in which teachers are active players in students' knowledge building (Copple et al., 1984).

Howard Gardner's theory of multiple intelligences (1983) widened our thinking about the diverse ways in which students successfully contribute to their own learning and to their communities. It validated the ways in which our school district defined success for individual students. Gardner's conceptualizations of human cognition in its many textures gave us a welcomed and accessible language to more fully understand and document student growth.

Learning to Reason Through Design

George Forman introduced us to the Reggio Emilia approach (Edwards et al., 1998), the well-respected approach to early childhood education developed in Italy after World War II by psychologist Loris Malaguzzi. Reggio teachers look at children as curious, self-initiating members of their community who work in partnership with others and the learning space to pursue meaning. They create schools with a common area called a piazza, often an indoor–outdoor space in which children have freedom to explore, and ateliers, studio spaces in which children work with each other and adults to invent products and representations of thinking. Our district's middle school was built on a similar model: The center of the school was the library through which everyone walked to get to other parts of the building, with the many art studios, shops, and spaces visibly adjacent. We had appreciated that the architecture was innovative and welcoming—now we were understanding its role in supporting relationships and enhancing the cognitive and affective development those relationships fostered.

Forman also introduced us to the pioneering thinkers and researchers working in the emerging world of computer technology, studying the effects of technology through the lens of developmental theory. Thirty-plus years ago, Forman and Pufall discussed the impact of technology in an edited book, *Constructivism in the Computer Age*, a description that still holds today:

> The miniaturization of memory storage devices, combined with inexpensive production techniques, has given the average person access to electronic tools for manipulating information and for representing events both physical and psychological. Just as paper and pencil make it possible to reason in ways that exceed the limits of our native short-term memory, so too the microcomputer may allow us to extend our cognitive reach into further unexplored territories. (Forman & Pufall, 1988, p. xi)

The first chapter in that book is authored by Seymour Papert, "The Conservation of Piaget: The Computer as Grist for the Constructivist Mill." Papert was a leader in introducing technology to children and researching how it affected their learning (1980, 1988). The psychologist Edith Ackerman, who worked with both Piaget and Papert, states:

> the difference is that Piaget's interest was mainly in the construction of internal stability (la conservation et la reorganisation des acquis), whereas Papert is more interested in the dynamics of change (la decouverte de nouveaute). (2001, p 8)

While Piaget focused on how children develop the mental structures that allow them to detach from concrete objects, grow to handle symbolic objects, and establish internal equilibration, Papert focused mainly on how children connect with technologies to learn and reason by constructing meaningful products. He called his work "constructionism" to validate the importance and lasting impact of creating artifacts outside of oneself. Papert's work on the ways in which children think about and interact with technology remains foundational to the field.

Mediation

Our expanding inquiries inevitably brought us to Lev Vygotsky (1962), who studied children's developing thinking in relation to social interactions and imaginative play, concluding that social learning precedes cognitive development. In seeking to understand the roles of culture and language in cognition, he used the groundbreaking dialectic method to look at transformations, a method in which he studied how word meaning and verbal thinking transformed over time and within the context of culture (Vygotsky, 1978). He came to understand language as a mediator in cognition, and he stressed the importance of scaffolding either by a teacher or older, more skillful peer as instrumental in children's cognitive development. This seemed inconsistent with what we had understood about language from Piaget's writing, so learning more about Vygotsky's work sent us back to Piaget (1923).

Piaget saw language development as linked to cognition that makes speech possible. A child may exclaim that she sees a flower. Her mother may say, "yes, it's a daisy," and the child may respond, "no, it's a flower." Until the child constructs the concept that a daisy is a type of flower, a daisy cannot simultaneously be a flower and a daisy. Although Piaget and Vygotsky offer different perspectives on the nature and development of speech and language, both views informed our pedagogy and practice, with Vygotsky offering more specific thoughts on pedagogical implications for special needs children (Mahn, 1999).

In studying Vygotsky and in thinking about children with special needs, we were drawn to a conference in New York City at which Reuven Feuerstein was the keynote speaker. Feuerstein was proposing a theory of structural cognitive modifiability, which stated that students' cognitive functioning can be modified by teachers mediating reasoning skills that are essentially content-free (Feuerstein et al., 1979/2002). The conference was oversold, and at lunch we ended up by chance sitting on the stairs next to Dr. Feuerstein, balancing sandwiches on our laps, "talking shop." We began to look at cognitive modifiability on a deeper level than we had previously understood. We were fascinated. Shortly thereafter, boxes of Feuerstein's Instrumental Enrichment Program arrived at our middle school and teachers began working with students on "organizing dots."

The Organization of Dots is one category of Feuerstein's Mediated Learning Experience tasks, asking students to study a cloud of dots and outline given figures within them. The experience invites students to identify patterns that are present but not obvious, which activates a variety of cognitive functions. Working with students this way added to our repertoire of teaching tools and deepened our understanding of cognitive mediation and curriculum negotiation.

Feuerstein's work also helped us develop a better appreciation of Vygotsky's conceptions of mediated learning. Vygotsky's first work published in English in 1962, well after his death in 1937, includes an introduction by the noted cognitive psychologist, Jerome Bruner, who wrote:

> I leave to the reader the delight of discovering Vygotsky's conception of intelligence as a capacity to benefit from instruction and his radical proposal that we test intelligence accordingly. (quoted in Vygotsky, 1962, p. viii)

The Cognitive Revolution

Bruner (1960), himself, was a key influencer, along with Noam Chomsky (1977, 2006), in the cognitive revolution that shifted thinking about how we view the human mind. Both see human beings as problem finding, problem solving, and logic seeking. Chomsky highlighted the role that logic plays in learning, particularly language learning, which he sees as innately wired but embedded in one's culture. Bruner studied curricula purposefully structured to promote the construction of knowledge. Both scholars see learning as a natural unfolding of biological capacities and teaching as a process of providing stimulating settings with worthwhile problems to solve and encouragement to seek truth and understanding. Looking at cognition as the capacity to benefit from instruction rather than being a static, fixed asset opens teachers to growth mindsets, such as the one revealed during that time by the New Zealand teacher, Sylvia Ashton-Warner (1963). She provided contextually rich stories of indigenous Maori children, struggling to learn through traditional British methods but successfully learning to read and write fluently through organic processes emerging from their connections with text meaningful to them. She concluded that the meaning of written and spoken stories is created by each child's interactions with teachers, peers, text, nature, and culture.

Constance Kamii (1993) has researched children's development of sociological and intellectual autonomy over decades. She has produced meticulous research on primary school children's numerical thinking. A demanding scholar, she helped us learn about the structures of numeracy. Consider the linking plastic cubes typically used in elementary school math instruction to represent relationships among "ones, tens, and hundreds" and instruction in "carrying" and "borrowing." Kamii (2011) has shown through numerous studies that most students do not build place value relationships from this type of instruction, yet the linking cubes remain prevalent in many elementary classrooms, and parents continue to teach "carrying" and "borrowing" at home if the classroom does not. Construction of new understandings is not dependent on access to physical objects that can be manipulated or direct instruction of algorithms—what matters is how students use materials and ideas in service to their own learning and how teachers set up the environment and mediate interactions.

Catherine Twomey Fosnot (1996, 2005) helped us unravel many of the complexities of constructivism as a theory of learning across disciplines, particularly offering insights into elementary school children's mathematical thinking (Fosnot & Dolk, 2001). Rheta DeVries and Christina Sales (2010) taught us about preschool children's unfolding understandings of physical science concepts, providing a framework applicable across ages. Rosalind Driver and colleagues (1994) contributed extensive research on the evolving ideas of children and adolescents as they grappled with living science and physical science processes and the properties of materials. We continue to build understandings on the foundations created by these revolutionaries and the ones yet to come.

Culture and Morality

The profound contributions of Paolo Freire and Henry Giroux led us to better understand the role that culture and morality play in the development of reasoning. The work of both scholars catapulted us into inquiries related to critical pedagogy and its role in establishing culturally responsive classrooms in which teachers and students learn together, appreciating the complexities of their shared experiences and cultures. Recognizing that classrooms are non-neutral, value-laden settings helped us unpack the ideas of power and privilege, essential topics throughout history but urgent as today's schools grapple with more effective ways of promoting social justice and diminishing institutional racism. Friere (1970/2000) wrote about transformations in society that are made possible by teachers who introduce new ideas related to societal class distinctions, and how these ideas are either supported or repressed by power. Both Giroux (2011) and Friere have helped us wrestle with distinguishing truth with an uppercase "T" from truth with a lowercase "t." Like many, we're still wrestling with that.

Friere and Giroux led us to Lawrence Kohlberg's studies on moral development (1981), whose research on the subject was centered entirely on young male subjects. Kohlberg led us to the research of his colleague, Carol Gilligan (1982), who put forth a theory of moral development in women. Both have contributed to the literature on how moral reasoning emerges. Nel Noddings's (1995) extensive writing on the role that reason and education play in the active construction of notions of justice helped us emphasize the ethics of caring in our work with students. Rheta DeVries and Betty Zan (2012) illustrated the processes by which teachers create sociomoral cultures and norms in early childhood classrooms, norms that can facilitate moral development. Their work along with the application of attachment theory in classroom settings that Marilyn Watson documented (2003) draw powerful images of how teachers' classroom interactions support children's ethical and intellectual growth in safe, engaging settings. Alfie Kohn (1993) helped us better understand the far-reaching role of competition in schools. His research documented the undeniable benefits of learning as its own reward and how external motivators interfere with the development of self-regulation.

Through his personal stories about the racial and residential segregation of poor children and children of color, Jonathan Kozol (1967) became another important voice for us, passing on his outrage over the systemic injustices embedded in America's schools. Predictably, children growing up in poverty typically attend schools with fewer resources and therefore fewer educational opportunities, often robbing students of their legal rights and creative spirits. These stories heightened our sensitivities to the ways in which teachers can also be advocates and activists.

Science of Learning

Research on the developmental, social, cultural, emotional, and cognitive components of learning has a long history. As research on these various dimensions of the human condition began to blend in the 1990s with new understandings of the functioning of the human brain, the term, science of learning, emerged.

Science of learning was popularized by the seminal publication *How People Learn* (NRC, 2000), edited by John Bransford, Ann Brown, and Rodney Cocking, which synthesized data from voluminous studies on concept formation and academic learning. In a follow-up publication, Suzanne Donovan and John Bransford, as editors of *How Students Learn* (NRC, 2005), collated numerous, vetted, practical teaching strategies associated with improved learning. In both volumes, the term "constructivist teaching" is used to describe the overall approach of the recommended frameworks. These texts and their follow-up texts portray learners as active, purposeful, motivated, and self-regulating, deploying metacognitive skills in solving problems, and utilizing prior knowledge and experience to make sense of new experiences. This is the constructivist definition of a learner.

The science of learning literature is clear and persuasive—constructivism explains much of how humans learn and why related teaching practices are successful. Constructivist teaching practices allow students to actively experience phenomena and adapt and organize their thinking. Adaptation and organization are essential to learning because they involve continually balancing and adjusting the processes of assimilation and accommodation, leading to cognitive equilibration, as Piaget's research demonstrates.

The American Psychological Association continues to support its long established 14 learner-centered principles as the enduring framework for school reform and design (Learner-Centered Principles Work Group of the American Psychological Association's Board of Educational Affairs, 1997). This framework emerges from a century of research studies on teaching and learning and aligns with constructivist learning theory (see summary in Figure 3.1).

Figure 3.1. APA's 14 Learner-Centered Principles

Cognitive and Metacognitive Factors

1. *Nature of the learning process.* The learning of complex subject matter is most effective when it is an intentional process of constructing meaning from information and experience.
2. *Goals of the learning process.* The successful learner, over time and with support and instructional guidance, can create meaningful, coherent representations of knowledge.
3. *Construction of knowledge.* The successful learner can link new information with existing knowledge in meaningful ways.
4. *Strategic thinking.* The successful learner can create and use a repertoire of thinking and reasoning strategies to achieve complex learning goals.
5. *Thinking about thinking.* Higher-order strategies for selecting and monitoring mental operations facilitate creative and critical thinking. Successful learners can reflect on how they think and learn, set reasonable learning or performance goals, select potentially appropriate learning strategies or methods, and monitor their progress toward these goals.
6. *Context of learning.* Learning is influenced by environmental factors, including culture, technology, and instructional practices. Learning does not occur in a vacuum.

Motivational and Affective Factors

7. *Motivational and emotional influences on learning.* What and how much is learned is influenced by the motivation. Motivation to learn, in turn, is influenced by the individual's emotional states, beliefs, interests and goals, and habits of thinking.
8. *Intrinsic motivation to learn.* The learner's creativity, higher-order thinking, and natural curiosity all contribute to motivation to learn.
9. *Effects of motivation on effort.* Acquisition of complex knowledge and skills requires extended learner effort and guided practice.

Developmental and Social Factors

10. *Developmental influences on learning.* As individuals develop, there are different opportunities and constraints for learning. Learning is most effective when differential development within and across physical, intellectual, emotional, and social domains is taken into account. Individuals learn best when material is appropriate to their developmental level and is presented in an enjoyable and interesting way.
11. *Social influences on learning.* Learning is influenced by social interactions, interpersonal relations, and communication with others.

Individual Differences Factors

12. *Individual differences in learning.* Learners have different strategies, approaches, and capabilities for learning that are a function of prior experience and heredity.
13. *Learning and diversity.* Learning is most effective when differences in learners' linguistic, cultural, and social backgrounds are taken into account.

(continued)

Figure 3.1. (*continued*)

14. *Standards and assessment.* Setting appropriately high and challenging standards and assessing the learner as well as learning progress—including diagnostic, process, and outcome assessment—are integral parts of the learning process.

These principles lend support to workshop approaches to writing, conceptually based mathematics programs, science and social studies courses structured around inquiry and argument, and teacher education that connects active learning and technology, all of which are aligned with constructivist principles.

In postsecondary institutions, pedagogical terms are less frequently used in describing educational programs, but there are a number of examples of college programs rooted in approaches aligned with constructivist pedagogy. Process-Oriented Guided Inquiry Learning (POGIL) is one of them. A student-centered, group-learning instructional strategy and philosophy that emerged from a study funded by the National Science Foundation (NSF), the model guides students through explorations to construct understanding, largely in STEM disciplines. A meta-analysis of 21 studies involving almost 8,000 students compared POGIL to standard lecture methods and found that POGIL doubled the numbers of students passing a class when compared to a standard lecture classroom, reducing the risk of failing by nearly 38%, and increasing the potential to retain more students in STEM disciplines (Walker & Warfa, 2017).

Science Education for New Civic Engagement and Responsibilities (SENCER), emerging from another NSF study, partners with colleges and universities to modify traditional courses or establish new ones that put student voice and engagement in global concerns at the center. Etkina and Mestra (2004) report that constructivist theory is the view of learning on which their SENCER-based faculty work proceeds. Other similar programs exist at the college level.

Universal Design for Learning

Our pantheon includes Ronald Mace. Needing to use a wheelchair after suffering childhood polio, he recognized the barriers that people with disabilities face. His advocacy on government committees prompted the Universal Design for Learning (UDL) movement that has become a primary framework for inclusive educational practice (Dolan & Hall, 2001). The UDL framework helps to make constructivist learning theory more visible, in practice and in rationale.

Originally designed to reduce physical barriers through architectural design, UDL grew to include curriculum design. It seeks to offer all students barrier-free, challenge-based curricula that value the voice of the learner (Pisha & Coyne, 2001). After emerging in the early 1980s as an approach to assist students with special needs, UDL soon became a framework with broader application. Its principles seek to activate the three brain networks known to be essential to learning: recognition, strategic, and affective (CAST, 2018). Teachers activate *recognition* networks of the brain by providing information and materials to students in multiple formats (e.g., texts on different reading levels, audio books, video segments); they activate *strategic* networks by encouraging students to share what they know in a variety of ways (e.g., create a skit, write a poem or expository essay, design an animated video); and they activate students' *affective* networks by offering problem-based challenging curricula that engage learners' interests and participation (e.g., the curriculum challenges and lessons discussed in Chapter 2).

UDL, as a framework for understanding learning through the activation of brain networks, complements Feuerstein's notion that the brain is malleable through mediated learning experiences, Piaget's notions that the brain reconstitutes itself through development, and Vygotsky's idea that learning occurs at the leading edge of students' cognitive development, all of which leads us to neuronal wiring and firing.

WIRING AND FIRING

Our journey into the whys and wherefores of learning began within a fascination with its biological underpinnings, and today's journey continues with the marvels of neuroscience. The notion that learning can change the physical brain, and in turn, that new neuronal pathways in the brain make new learning possible has been accepted for decades (Hebb, 1949) in the neuroscientific community, but is a fairly new construct in education. Epstein's intriguing hypothesis in the 1970s that brain size explained cognitive spurts proved to be inaccurate, but the plasticity of the brain and its growth from webs of neural wirings and firings, confirmed by more sophisticated research over the last decades, is offering explanatory data to developmental theories of learning.

Although neuroscientists cannot yet explain the underlying cellular or molecular events that enable the brain to sculpt itself from learning, the fact that it does is well documented, and it is exciting and confirmatory. Although the transfer of research from the neuroscience community to instruction is in its infancy, neuroscientific understandings of how the physical brain works are providing biological explanations for constructivism. Neural constructivism is the domain of neuroscience that studies how the brain allows environmental factors to shape its structure and function (Quartz & Sejnowski, 1997).

Ramachandran (2011) studies how mirror neurons, specifically, contribute to understanding social behavior. We see this research as providing beginning explanations of how Feuerstein's mediating learning works. Mirror neurons enable people to mimic behavior and refine social skills and are thought to be related to the development of empathy. Feuerstein, in speaking about his mediated learning projects, says:

> The mirror neurons are the main, but not the only, mechanism for the ability of the brain to be modified by experience. Plasticity works throughout the brain and throughout our lifetimes . . . it is the linkage between the neural plasticity and the mediated learning experience that makes this possible. (Feuerstein et al., 2010, p. 138)

In many ways, the work of the developmental psychologists and educators discussed in this chapter presaged today's burgeoning field of neuroscience. Piaget, a biologist before his career as a genetic epistemologist studying the nature of knowledge, saw all living organisms as self-regulating. "For Piaget, adaptation is . . . a dynamic, ongoing process in which the hereditary structure of the organism interacts with the external environment in such a way as to reconstitute itself for better survival" (Pulaski, 1980, p. 9). Many researchers of development and pedagogy today view learning as a process of adaptive construction involving both the biology of the brain–mind and the experiences of the learner. Brain-imaging data support the central notion proffered by Piaget in his earliest work, as well as the ideas of others—that learning produces increasingly intricate networks of neural structures, and increasingly intricate networks of neural structures produce more learning.

In the words of Siegel: "The mind uses the brain to create itself" (2010, p. 261).

The brain–mind connection is a duality (Fischer, 2009). Anatomical change in the brain is associated with developmentally provocative experiences and/or perception of discrepancies, both of which are intellectual clashes between what a learner would predict based on prior knowledge and what is perceived in the moment.

> The brain is the source of behavior, but in turn it is modified by the behaviors it produces. This dynamic loop between brain structure and brain function is at the root of the neural basis of cognition, learning and plasticity. (Zatorre et al., 2012, p. 528)

The brain's amazing capacity to change and reorganize itself demonstrates that intelligence is not fixed. Yet, we often hear, "You're smart," rather than "You persevered," or "You're a great athlete," rather than "That footwork enabled you to break free for a basket." Neuroscience affirms for teachers that speaking to students about behaviors is more useful and accurate than evaluative statements about perceived attributes.

Dennick (2016) reports:

> the importance of active learning methods, as recommended by constructivist pedagogy, is supported by studies of neurogenesis in the adult brain. Neurogenesis continually occurs in the dentate gyrus area of the hippocampus of the human brain, a region well known for its part in learning and memory. Furthermore it is now established from mouse models that activity in an enriched living environment stimulates neurogenesis and results in increased synaptic connectivity. The implication of these and other studies suggests that learning is a physically constructive process in the brain which is enhanced by active learning. (para. 27)

The synergy between neuroscience and theories of cognitive growth supports the importance of classroom settings that foster self-regulation.

OPENING NEW DOORS TO SELF-REGULATION

Self-regulation is an essential component of learning. For Piaget, the developing capacities to act with intention, organize thinking, and control impulses describe the self-regulation that makes cognitive equilibrium possible. For Vygotsky, private inner speech and speech with others aid the development of self-regulating behaviors within the context of culture. In a newer area of psychology generating significant interest today, mindfulness refers to the self-regulating processes by which people awaken their senses and look with new eyes at present experiences.

Mindfulness

Mindfulness is a field of study that is revealing dispositions and practices that heighten or dampen neural activity in various parts of the brain. Most well-known through research reported in medical journals within the health services community (Kabat-Zinn, 2013), mindfulness is growing in its applications to school settings (Zenner et al., 2014) and global organizations (Sutcliffe et al., 2016). It is a practice of intentionally focusing the mind on an object, place, or phenomenon while releasing worry and judgment about issues beyond that immediate focus. It is a practice that cultivates the noticing of one's responses to external and internal stimuli of the moment.

Essential components of mindfulness practice include a set of attitudes: acceptance, by inclining toward meeting experiences with an open mind; patience, by releasing expectations; beginner's mind, by looking through new eyes; trust, by valuing one's strength; and nonjudgment, by impartially acknowledging experiences. Focusing on the sensation of breathing is a frequently traveled path toward cultivating these mindful attitudes while developing one's capacity for stable attention.

Studies of changes in the brain with mindful breathing indicate increased neural activity in the prefrontal cortex of the brain (Tang et al., 2015; Valk et al., 2017), although underlying neural mechanisms related to this increase still remain unclear. These changes in the brain potentially enhance one's capacity to respond to situations with heightened self-regulation, rather than engaging in knee-jerk reactions stemming from the limbic parts of our brains. This capacity, known as the inhibitory response, is a key factor in executive functioning, the set of mental processes that allow us to control our own behavior, also called self-regulation. "Executive functioning" is a term used widely in neuropsychology, while "self-regulation" is the analogous term used most often in cognitive developmental psychology.

The prefrontal cortex that controls most self-regulation is particularly malleable during adolescence. This plasticity of the teenage brain makes mindfulness experiences in adolescence particularly valuable for personal fulfillment and academic success. Short-term mindful breath awareness inhibits impulsivity, such as that associated with substance abuse or overeating (Pozuelos & Malinowski, 2019). Mindful breathing can develop one's capacity to hold back habitual responses that can unravel one's well-being. The practice can help replace automatic, often unproductive behavior with mediated, empowering responses (Gallant, 2016). Early research on adolescent brains validates the merit of classroom practices that foster self-regulation and advocates for explicit classroom attention to promoting it (Blakemore, 2018; Flook et al., 2010).

Mindfulness in Classrooms

Mindfulness informs constructivist educators seeking to adapt curriculum to meet students in the moment and at their current levels of functioning (DeRuy, 2016). The work of Dweck (2007) fits in here, as well. Teachers with a growth mindset, a belief in students' capacities to change, are more likely to engage students in activities that provoke learning than teachers with a fixed mindset—a belief that students' capacities to learn are essentially unchangeable.

Figure 3.2 illustrates the relationship between mindful attitudes and constructivist teaching practices. The connection is striking.

With its quiet tone, mindfulness enables people of all ages to develop a deeper understanding of their own learning. A teacher who can appreciate her own beginner's mind can help students appreciate their individual beginners' minds, which invites them to pause, ask more direct questions,

Figure 3.2. Mindful Attitudes and Constructivist Educator Practices

Mindfulness Attitudes	Constructivist Educator Practices
Acceptance—inclining toward meeting experiences with an open mind	• Meeting students at their present functioning level • Seeking to understand and value their thinking
Patience—allowing things to unfold in their own time, appreciating the need to "pause"	• Acknowledging and responding to age-appropriate progressions • Seeking to understand and honor students' developmental readiness • Allowing for wait time
Beginner's mind—looking at the world anew, with open curiosity	• Recognizing that solving problems nourishes the mind • Challenging students with meaningful questions, authentic problems, and pattern disruptions • Honoring the importance of "reinventing the wheel"
Trust—valuing one's own authority	• Recognizing the inner authority of students; encouraging students to trust their emerging capacities
Nonjudgment—impartially witnessing one's experiences	• Approaching students without judgment • Replacing evaluation with descriptive assessment

participate more confidently with open minds, and engage more fully in the moment. This helps students see schoolwork as more relevant.

When teachers view themselves as learners, engage with big ideas, and ask questions with which they themselves still grapple, students witness powerful images of productive, rich adulthood. These images shape their perceptions of the positive value of school and work and who they are and can become (Csikszentmihalyi & Schneider, 2008).

IMAGES OF LEARNERS

In concluding this sprint through the thinking, research, and practice of the scholars who influenced our thinking, we harken back to Socrates, whose dialectic method of teaching engaged his pupils in transforming ideas into larger conceptions. A quote attributed to Socrates—"I cannot teach anybody anything. I can only make them think"—captures how many great teachers approach their work.

We wondered about the first person to use the word "constructivism." Our research brought us to the philosopher Giambattista Vico (1710). The psychologist Ernst von Glasersfeld interprets Vico as having stated: "the human mind can only know what the human mind has made" (1990, p. 3).

As public school educators, we want to acknowledge Horace Mann (1852), who, in the mid-1800s, advocated a system of free, public education in the United States intended to prepare children for their role as thoughtful, engaged citizens. Mann was a progressive thinker during a segregationist era whose compelling vision for education in a democratic society resonates with principles of constructivism and continues to inspire in today's fraught climate.

And, of course, it would be impossible not to acknowledge the transformative work of John Dewey (1900), who described education as ideally honoring wonder, curiosity, and the right to make mistakes, all of which are linked to the individual's internal construction of knowledge. Dewey urged schools not to focus solely on the preparation of students for adulthood, but also to honor the lives that students lead as children. Dewey called for schooling to be "a process of living and not a preparation for future living" (1938/1997), a view that complements the mindfulness focus on living and learning fully in the present. Dewey's quote also corresponds with emerging insights from neuroscience: the duality that experience grows the physical brain and the physical brain grows one's capacities to perceive. Understandably, the more educators tend to "today" with students, the more they prepare students for "tomorrow."

Like Mann, Dewey saw educating students to be thinkers and informed citizens as central to the sustenance of a strong democracy. Although Dewey's work did not have a noticeable impact on mainstream education during his time, Lucy Sprague Mitchell (1916) was highly influenced by him and applied his notions about learning to the creation of learner-centered teacher education programs to support his approach in schools.

Collectively, the work of these scholars coalesces to create images of learners as constructors of knowledge and schools as laboratories for learning. We honor these beacons, along with so many other scholars, too many to mention here, who have and continue to contribute to our thinking about pedagogy.

This chapter concludes Part I of this book. Part II, Guiding Principles, looks deeper into teaching as a conceptual art. It explores principles and practices of constructivist pedagogy that use national frameworks to guide curricula selections and instructional decisions. It describes how to frame teaching with big ideas and design thinking, steer lessons with transdisciplinary strategies, and assess student learning responsibly with multiple measures that capture important outcomes.

PART I: MAKING THE CASE FOR CONSTRUCTIVIST SCHOOLS	
Chapter 1 Imagining Schools as . . .	Schools moving to their next level of work open up thinking about teaching and learning, open new ways of understanding student performance, open discussions about how success is defined, open students' minds to the wonders of the worlds in which they live, and open students' hearts to ethical engagement in those worlds.
Chapter 2 Transforming Schools From the Inside Out	Teachers who transform their practice through reflection on assumptions, processes, and outcomes transform the schools in which they work.
Chapter 3 Searching for Meaning	Educational, psychological, and neuroscientific research coalesce into a compelling view of human learning that argues strongly for a constructivist approach to schooling.

Part II

GUIDING PRINCIPLES

CHAPTER 4

Tying the Learning Frameworks Together

Separately and together, the frameworks of national learning standards recognize learners as self-regulating beings seeking to construct understandings of their worlds. Social studies, English, science, math, the many arts, world languages, library science, and health and physical education are typically separate departments in schools with their own specific content. At the middle and high school levels, these subjects are taught by separate faculties with different certifications. Although the content is different, these subjects share similar core approaches to problem solving, inquiry, critical thinking, and self-regulation. Recognizing these similarities enables teachers to engage students as thinkers across disciplines.

These frameworks represent transferable, unifying, overarching ideas and processes for guiding classroom instruction and school organization. This chapter presents the national learning frameworks of eight disciplines through six classrooms engaged in transdisciplinary work.

In the era of testing and accountability, standards have come to play a much larger role in schooling, sometimes with positive results and sometimes not. Although many dispute the usefulness and impact of standards, the often-overlooked frameworks on which national standards are based provide teachers with foundational ways of thinking about the concepts and content they teach. Standards and frameworks are often conflated, but they are very different. Standards describe content knowledge. Frameworks describe ways of thinking that allow students to build content knowledge.

Frameworks include the intellectual tools of each discipline, are conceptual in nature, and frame the core content of each set of standards, which are the topics and big ideas of the subject-bound curriculum. School districts often marginalize the frameworks by privileging content objectives directly linked to tests over intellectual tools or academic practices that lead to the development of concepts and skills. Minimizing the tools and practices of thinking about content ironically diminishes the likelihood of reaching content objectives. This is why teachers understanding the frameworks and knowing how to apply them are so important.

The following classrooms use frameworks from multiple disciplines. However, we use each classroom to highlight the framework of just one discipline.

We introduce the mathematics learning framework through a class trying to float some boats.

MATH: WHAT BOATS AND MEDICINES CAN TEACH US

Mr. Mwangi's 6th-grade math class is measuring aluminum foil to cut a piece that cannot exceed 72 square inches. The students are trying to make boats that will carry the greatest mass of a cargo of medicines up a river. They want to create a model boat, but the math of accurately cutting a piece of aluminum foil to the right size is their first challenge, a big challenge, a bigger challenge than Mr. Mwangi had anticipated. Mr. Mwangi intentionally limits the area of foil to require *measurement* of sides and promotes *decisionmaking* about shape. The students *persevere* through *trials and changes*, while Mr. Mwangi promotes *mathematical modeling* and *attention to precision* by asking about the boats' lengths and widths and the cargo's mass. Mr. Mwangi asks for students' mathematical *reasoning* behind their experimentation.

Mr. Mwangi incorporates aluminum foil, a pile of weights, and a trough of water into great teaching. Mr. Mwangi's lesson is an apt introduction to the mathematics frameworks.

Practices of Mathematics

The *practices* of the National Council of Teachers of Mathematics (NCTM) enable students to be mathematicians generating conceptual understanding and developing computational skills.

Let's look at a more straightforward math question: What is the sum of $10 + 20 + 30 + 40 + 50 + 60 + 70 + 80 + 90$? Students from classrooms in which math is taught as a search for patterns and an invention of procedures first look at the numbers in the problem to determine if they can identify an efficient strategy. A student's determination of which strategy to use is an executive functioning skill that involves decisionmaking as well as flexible mathematical skills. In these classrooms, there are multiple approaches. Some students

- use a "making hundreds" approach ($10 + 90 = 100$, $20 + 80 = 100$, $30 + 70 = 100$, $40 + 60 = 100$, plus one 50) and generate 450; or
- count how many groups of 20 exist (20), generate a subtotal (400), then add 10 for every odd number (5) to generate $400 + 50 = 450$; or

- reason that since there are an odd number of items that differ from each other by the same value, they could multiply the number of items in the sequence (9) by the middle number of the sequence (50) to get the sum: $9 \times 50 = 450$. (These students assert that it will always work, and they experiment with new sets of numbers. It works!)

These strategies are different than those used by students educated through more traditional math lessons. Students in these classes usually start at the left and procedurally use the standard addition algorithm to find a total of 450. Students in both of the above classrooms can generate an accurate sum. One group of students learns to apply a known procedure for addition problems, and the other group constructs new (to them) strategies. One approach requires repetition of a familiar procedure, while the other approach requires a search for patterns and decisionmaking.

After practice with implementing accepted procedures, students taught through more traditional lessons often become flummoxed when the problems look different or are changed in some way. For example, many of these students view subtraction problems as quite different from addition problems, requiring a different procedure. Students in conceptually based classes learn to flexibly apply multiple strategies across different representations of the same type of problem and come to see addition and subtraction as related procedures. Thus, their conceptual knowledge is often more transferable to novel situations.

Returning to the problem posed above, students in the "math as a search of patterns" class use many of the practices of the Common Core State Standards for Mathematics (National Governors Association, 2010) in finding the sum of the 10s from 10 to 90. Mr. Mwangi's class does, too. Figure 4.1 lists these practices.

These are the practices of mathematicians. These are the practices of students in Mr. Mwangi's class. These practices also correspond to the practices and ways of thinking of scientists. Ms. Ramble's class introduces the science learning framework.

Figure 4.1. Practices of the Math Frameworks

- Make sense of problems and persevere in solving them.
- Reason abstractly and quantitatively.
- Construct viable arguments and critique the reasoning of others.
- Model with mathematics.
- Use appropriate tools strategically.
- Attend to precision.
- Look for and make use of structure.
- Look for and express regularity in repeated reasoning.

Available at http://www.corestandards.org/Math/Practice.

SCIENCE: WHAT ANTS CAN TEACH US

Ms. Ramble's 4th-grade class watches ants carry crumbs across the sidewalk. Ms. Ramble invites the students to write poems about what they are seeing. While students compose their poems, Ms. Ramble provokes their thinking: Did they want to write about the size of the ant relative to the size of the crumb (pointing students to consider *scale*), might they enjoy writing about how far the ants travel (pointing students to consider *quantity*), how about writing about the role of body parts in transporting the crumb (relating *structure* and *function*), or maybe they wonder how the ants found the crumbs in the first place (*cause and effect*), or, or, or. Ms. Ramble intentionally focuses her students on the crosscutting concepts of science and the practices of science and engineering while simultaneously fostering the literacies of poetry writing.

Students in Ms. Ramble's class also watch where different fish in the class aquarium spend their time and write letters asking the fish questions about their neighborhoods. Her students write directions for another class on how a windup toy works. They observe the custodial crew salt the walkways during an afternoon snowfall and take notes about what they witness. In all cases, Ms. Ramble guides them in seeing, using, and thinking about patterns, making connections, and becoming engaged and challenged. Ms. Ramble incorporates ants, fish, windup toys, and snowfalls into great teaching.

Crosscutting Concepts and Practices of Science

The *crosscutting concepts* of the Next Generation Science Standards (National Research Council, 2013) are ways of thinking, also called intellectual tools. The science and engineering *practices* are activities that engage students in the work of scientists and engineers. Figure 4.2 lists these intellectual tools and practices.

Similar to the other frameworks, the crosscutting concepts apply across disciplines. Each is felt in our daily life experiences—for example, systems thinking, a way of thinking that applies across contents. Wolves, elks, willow trees, beavers, and rivers are part of an amazingly dynamic *ecosystem* in Yellowstone Park. They live together as parts of a grand *system*. In a different context, plane routes are part of a global transportation *system*. To travel from New York to Atlanta, you might need to change planes in Baltimore. In a third context, stringed, brass, woodwind, and percussion instruments play a piece by Tchaikovsky as part of an orchestral *system*. The examples are endless. Getting better at *systems thinking* helps all teachers, administrators, parents, and students in a school *system* understand issues and address thorny problems.

Similarly, *structure and function* relationships are embedded in activities across contents: writing a novel, discerning weather patterns, tracing

Figure 4.2. Crosscutting Concepts and Science and Engineering Practices of the Next Generation Science Standards

Crosscutting Concepts

- Looking for patterns
- Deciphering cause-and-effect relationships
- Recognizing the relevance of scale and proportion as quantities change
- Engaging in systems thinking
- Tracking how energy and matter flow within systems
- Determining how structure and function relate
- Considering how stability and change affect a system

Available at https://ngss.nsta.org/CrosscuttingConceptsFull.aspx.

Science and Engineering Practices

- Asking questions
- Developing and using models
- Planning and carrying out investigations
- Analyzing and interpreting data
- Using mathematics and computational thinking
- Constructing explanations
- Engaging in argument from evidence
- Obtaining, evaluating, and communicating information

Available at https://ngss.nsta.org/PracticesFull.aspx.

economic policies, developing therapeutic medicines, analyzing the features of animal body shapes, and developing architectural plans. *Structure and function* relationships also emerge in the repurposing of classroom space and the selecting of furniture of different designs, sizes, and materials. As schools respond to the global pandemic in ways that optimize space for social distancing, *structure and function* are critical considerations in decisionmaking.

The five other crosscutting concepts are also part of everyday life:

- The design of wearable fashion uses *scale and proportion* to dazzle and surprise. In international conflict, when countries discuss retaliation for perceived wrongdoings, they also grapple with determining *a proportional* response, while a student reading a poem and making meaning from an analogy or a simile also is thinking *proportionally*.
- We search for *patterns* in fields as diverse as global commercial trends and local bookstore sales, and in analyzing results of political polls.
- We weigh *cause and effect* when making many personal or economic decisions.

- We consider how *changing* one ingredient in a recipe or *changing* the location of an object can *change* the whole enterprise. We evaluate missed opportunity costs, or benefits, when choosing to keep something the *same.*
- We realize that *matter and energy* are interconnected ways of looking at our world when we see a seed become a plant.

When teachers use these terms and words, they invite students to use them as well. They direct students to ways of thinking that are useful as they reflect on their worlds, inside and outside of school, and search to better understand the swirl of phenomena around them. These are the crosscutting concepts of scientists, engineers, technologists, and health professionals.

The social studies framework is worded differently but has much in common with the math and science frameworks. Ms. Henry's class illustrates some of the commonalities.

SOCIAL STUDIES: WHAT HUCKLEBERRIES CAN TEACH US

It's early September in the Pacific Northwest, and students in Ms. Henry's 8th-grade social studies class are making huckleberry jam from the wild berries they picked at the edge of the school property. Huckleberries are native in the region, and Ms. Henry has organized this activity as part of the *people, places, and environments* theme of the social studies frameworks. She brings in nearby *producers* and *merchants* to compare their processes with the class's jam-making process, and to serve as reliable *resources* for addressing the students' emerging questions.

Ms. Henry's plans include investigating the aspects of the *geographical region* that enable huckleberries to grow there, and uses the class's own jam making as an anchor to explore the big ideas that we *produce* what we need or enjoy, we find ways to *transport* what we make to other people, and we help other people *use* what we make. This is simple language for the complex social studies theme of *production, distribution, and consumption.* Producing and distributing huckleberry jam helps students to make sense of this process. Students study the order and components of the jam making process, search for patterns as they wonder if the blue ones are sweeter than the red ones and wonder whether the berries ripen at the same time every year, and discuss quantity as they compute how many huckleberries make one jar of jam.

Culturally, huckleberries, known for their medicinal value, are one of the most important foods to Native People of the Pacific Northwest. They are high in antioxidants, good for diabetics, and ease a number of maladies. Making jam provides Ms. Henry's students the opportunity to experience the *culture and language* of people indigenous to their region. The unit also invites students into the visual arts, graphic design, and media arts of packaging and advertising, and opens conversations about native plants, and wild versus cultivated crops. Ms. Henry incorporates huckleberries into great teaching.

Themes of Social Studies

The *themes* of the National Council for the Social Studies (2010) categorize the human experience into broad ways of thinking about large and important ideas in history, geography, anthropology, and the other domains of the social sciences. These themes are listed in Figure 4.3.

Van Hover and Hicks (2017) find that much research on student learning in social studies rests on and informs constructivist principles. They write:

> We argued that social constructivism is often the penumbra—the shadow—that implicitly frames or undergirds research on student learning in social studies, but is rarely named, unpacked and explored in an explicit, in-depth manner. . . . While certain concepts and theoretical frameworks continue to be contested—and to evolve—we also recognize that there are key learning principles (synthesized from social (dialectical) constructivism and research in cognitive psychology) that are well supported by research in the field of cognitive psychology. And many of these principles—explicitly and implicitly—are the "shadows" that shape and are shaped by social studies research studies on student learning. (pp. 273–274)

Teachers who address these themes provoke thinking and discussions about sociopolitical, humanitarian, and social justice issues as well as the dates, names, and eras that situate the larger issues into chronological time. For example, the murders of Ahmaud Arbery, Breonna Taylor, Elijah McClain, and George Floyd occurred during the pandemic of 2020, igniting massive protests throughout the United States and abroad. Their deaths are connected to the killing of Eric Garner and Sandra Bland and Philando

---

Figure 4.3. Themes of the Social Studies Framework

- Culture
- Time, continuity, and change
- People, places, and environments
- Individual development and identity
- Individuals, groups, and institutions
- Power, authority, and governance
- Production, distribution, and consumption
- Science, technology, and society
- Global connections
- Civic ideals and practices

Available at https://www.socialstudies.org/standards/national-curriculum-standards-social-studies-introduction.

Castile and Tamir Rice and Freddy Gray and Michael Brown and Trayvon Martin. Their deaths are connected to the deaths of Addie Mae Collins, Cynthia Wesley, Carole Robertson, and Darol Denise McNair, and their deaths are connected to the deaths of Emmett Till and George Stinney Jr., and their deaths are connected to the murder of numerous other Black citizens, which ultimately are traceable back to the enslavement of Black people over 400 years ago, the civil war that was fought over that enslavement, and the personal and systemic racism that grew from that enslavement. Themes provide a home for names and dates and events and place them in context. The theme of "power, authority, and governance" can frame the lessons that discuss and analyze these deaths, as can "civic ideals and practices."

The social studies framework that describes the unifying themes of social scientists and historians speaks to many of the same cognitive structures and practices as the frameworks of other disciplines and applies across cultures and throughout students' academic careers.

The social studies framework connects to language arts—and other frameworks—in its quest to stimulate broad communication and global connections. Ms. Davis's class provides a window.

LITERACY: WHAT ARTIFACTS CAN TEACH US

In Ms. Davis's 9th-grade English class, students are journalists at a "dig site," which, in this classroom, are shallow containers of sand and soil with buried artifacts. Students explore their site by carefully unearthing the artifacts with brushes and tools, tracking the type and location of their *evidence* in notebooks or tablets, and *constructing a plausible story* about what might have happened at the site centuries ago. Working in pairs, the students agree on a way to excavate so they can record their findings accurately and coauthor a reasonable, evidence-based story. In this expository writing lesson, students work as journalists and illustrators, but also engage in the work of archeologists and historians.

To prompt richer investigative reporting, Ms. Davis fosters *collaborative problem solving* and seeks to *strengthen independent thought* with questions such as "Do the unearthed objects have any characteristics in common?" and "You have found many broken objects. Are there any clues as to why that may be?" She approaches other student groups with: "How many objects did you find? Is there a relationship between the number of objects and where you found them?" Other students are given other questions to contemplate: "Some of the objects you found seem so different from the objects in our world today. Can you determine what they were used for and how they worked?" In this lesson, Ms. Davis helps students *analyze and evaluate information* and attend to the *ethical responsibilities* of using evidence to interpret results and form conclusions.

After Ms. Davis's student journalists write their articles about their findings at the class "dig site," they write and share poems inspired by the artifacts. Ms. Davis then introduces *To Be of Use* by Marge Piercy (1982) and asks students to consider the poet's perspectives on artifacts such as Hopi vases, Greek amphoras, and water pitchers. Ms. Davis invites her class into enlarging their perspectives and diversifying the genres they use to express their thinking. Ms. Davis incorporates sand, artifacts, brushes, rolls of string, and poetry into great teaching.

Literacies of Language Arts

The *literacies* of the National Council of Teachers of English (NCTE, 2019) go beyond reading, writing, listening, and speaking. They speak to today's evolving social, cultural and communicative practices. They call for alignment in curriculum, assessment, and teaching practice. The literacies are listed in Figure 4.4.

Many of these literacies are addressed in Ms. Davis's class using simple nonelectronic tools and technologies. In other lessons, Ms. Davis uses multimedia tools and platforms for virtual meetings and online exchanges with students in partnership schools in other parts of the world. NCTE invites teachers to consider expanded definitions of "text" in a digital world (NCTE, 2018). The council recommends teaching students the principles of design; exposing students to theories connected to issues of power and representation in the arts; introducing students to the idea of audience that reaches beyond the classroom; and asking students to create multimodal mashups and explore other emerging media genres, as a few examples among many. These activities not only build technological prowess, but they also empower students to design and share information for global communities and develop skills to manage multiple streams of simultaneous information and evaluate multimedia texts.

Figure 4.4. Literacies of the Language Arts Framework

- Develop proficiency and fluency with the tools of technology.
- Build intentional cross-cultural connections and relationships with others so to pose and solve problems collaboratively and strengthen independent thought.
- Design and share information for global communities to meet a variety of purposes.
- Manage, analyze, and synthesize multiple streams of simultaneous information.
- Create, critique, analyze, and evaluate multimedia texts.
- Attend to the ethical responsibilities required by these complex environments.

Available at ncte.org/library/NCTEFiles/Resources/Positions/Framework_21stCent _Curr_Assessment.pdf.

These literacies are universal and, like the other frameworks, are not unique to school learning. They are part of everyday life. For example, visitors to the Museo de la Memoria y los Derechos Humanos (Museum of Memory and Human Rights) in Santiago, Chile, are asked to ponder questions within an exhibit:

- Can science tell us anything about racism?
- There are different breeds of dogs, so why shouldn't there be different races of humans?
- If races don't exist, then why do people have different skin color?
- Do our geographical origins make us genetically very different?
- One hundred years from now, will we all be of mixed heritage?
- We all come from Africa, right?

In thinking about and discussing the questions, visitors think about the nature of global communities and sources of information and ponder ethical issues.

These are the literacies of citizens, writers, speakers, readers, and listeners. They connect to the arts framework, and Mr. Petrauskas's class helps to illustrate these core art processes.

THE ARTS: WHAT WINDY DAYS CAN TEACH US

In Mr. Petrauskas's 11th-grade art class, students are engaged in studying kinetic art and its connections to the wind and sun. One group of students decides to build wind sculptures that also serve as anemometers. Mr. Petrauskas encourages their designs and prompts discussions about patterns, including extreme weather patterns that are becoming more frequent and are changing habitats around the globe.

As students design their anemometers, Mr. Petrauskas invites them to consider the artistry of the final sculpture while attending to the engineering of weather instruments. All of the final pieces *created* by the students look very different from one another. Mr. Petrauskas organizes individual presentations, enabling students to *share* their original art that *connects* science/technology/society, develop and practice *communication* skills, *produce* devices that delight the senses while also serving to indicate windspeed, and *respond* to each other's creations. Mr. Petrauskas incorporates windy and sunny days into great teaching.

Processes of the Arts

The National Core Arts Standards (National Coalition for Core Arts Standards, 2015) represent the creative journeys of dance, media, music,

Figure 4.5. Processes of the National Core Arts

Creating	Performing, Presenting, Producing	Responding	Connecting

Available at https://www.nationalartsstandards.org.

theater, and visual arts. The framework focuses on conceptual understanding of the *processes* in which artists of all media engage. Figure 4.5 represents the categories of artistic processes.

The framework promotes the notion that students conceive, develop, and respond to original art; that dance, music, theater, visual art, and media arts all involve performance, presentation, and production; that students make meaning from responding to art; and that students connect art to personal experiences and/or societal contexts and, by doing so, build new understandings of phenomena, people, objects, and ideas.

Think about Picasso's famous 1923 quote: "Art is a lie that makes us realize truth . . ."(in Barr, 1946, p. 270). It is the artist who conceives the performance, product, or presentation, and the viewers who interpret it through their unique experiential lens. A similar scenario can describe a classroom: A teacher conceives and presents what is important to know while each student interprets it uniquely. The teacher understands that interactions with students begin with their present conceptions as launching points for further study. These are the processes of artists, musicians, dancers, and performers.

Let's visit Mr. Lopez's class in order to introduce the frameworks for world languages, libraries, and health and physical education.

LANGUAGE, LIBRARIES, HEALTH:
WHAT ROCKS AND WATER CAN TEACH US

Mr. Lopez's bilingual 8th-grade earth science class of native Spanish speakers learning English is studying aquifers—underground rock layers filled with water that flows through them. The students are looking at water storage and the rate at which water flows through different layers of different-sized rocks. In the current unit of study, students are consistently reporting lab results that surprise Mr. Lopez—because the results are different from previous years' results and thus different from his expectation. Mr. Lopez discusses the findings with his colleagues and learns that they are reporting similar confusion about lab results in their classes. In response, the entire science department faculty launches its own investigation, seeking to discover why their students are getting the same "wrong" results.

At some point, one of the teachers realizes that the students are using rocks from a new vendor, purchased for the first time this year. Teachers and students together examine not only the composition and size of the rocks, but the impact of rock shape on the water storage capacity and the water flow rates of the mass of rocks.

Teachers prompt discussions on ways to keep *track of data, find and use resources*, and *cite evidence* in *forging arguments* and *communicating findings*. As students and teachers work together as co-investigators, the world language goals of *communication* become the heart of the classroom. Mr. Lopez had seen a *pattern*—the students were getting the same "wrong" answer. But, the word "pattern" in English is used differently than "*el patron*" in Spanish. What did Mr. Lopez mean? Students and Mr. Lopez began speaking in Spanish to clarify. They analyzed the word and the meanings in both languages and advanced their proficiency in both. They created a *community of learners* engaged in the purposeful communication of clarifying the terms being used while studying the issues involved in the water flow problem.

Students witnessed their teachers engaging in the same processes that they encourage in students. The teachers were amazed that the shape of rocks had such a significant influence on water flow. Their inquiry addressed a puzzlement. As curious thinkers, Mr. Lopez and his colleagues consulted library resources and engaged in problem solving. They engaged in these processes for their own learning, and they modeled it for their students. Mr. Lopez and his colleagues incorporate rocks, water, and bewilderments into great teaching.

Goals of World Languages

Mr. Lopez's class pursues clear communication within their culturally responsive, community responsive, collaborative classroom. The learning *goals* of the World-Readiness Standards for Learning Languages (National Standards Collaborative Board, 2015) place communication at the heart of human experience. The American Council on the Teaching of Foreign Languages developed these goals to guide schools in preparing students to be linguistically and culturally ready to function as world citizens. The council refers to its goals as the 5-C's, shown in Figure 4.6.

This framework takes a broad view of language learning, situating it beyond the classroom and valuing it as essential to enhancing global competence, personal experience, and life and career options. In pursuing fluency in a new language, learners interact with each other in the new language to make meaning.

Expanding artful and careful *communication* is the first goal of language learning. Heritage speakers may share family recipes. American Sign Language learners may sign baking instructions. Learners use the new language to engage with the products of the *culture* and examine it from new

Figure 4.6. Goals for Language Learning

Communication
Cultures
Comparisons
Connections
Communities

Available at https://www.actfl.org.

perspectives. Learners can prepare menus for restaurants they create, cooking with ingredients indigenous to the culture and narrating the culinary techniques to diners. Learners make *connections* with disciplinary topics by using the new language in solving problems. How to adjust a recipe by halving each ingredient requires not only number sense but the learning of numbers in the new language. Learners *compare* the new language to their own—searching for patterns in numbers, searching for patterns in word endings, and searching for patterns in syntax and grammar, in general, expanding the understanding of both languages. Learners use the new language in multilingual *communities* and become a new multilingual community. Teachers encourage students to forge bonds with communities speaking the new language, both locally and through Internet connections, enlarging the sphere that students call their community. The tribe grows.

These are the goals of diplomats, interpreters, tour guides, and global businesspeople. The library frameworks complement these goals.

Shared Foundations of Libraries

Today's school libraries have stretched far beyond places to find books. They are multimedia systems of infinite resources and research options. For students to effectively use these resources, the American Library Association (2018) has developed a Standards Framework for Learners consisting of *domains* that develop the competencies to think, create, share, and grow and *key commitments* to practice that invite students to inquire, include, collaborate, curate, explore, and engage. See Figure 4.7.

These shared foundations invite teachers to create learning opportunities applicable in any discipline. Learners *inquire* by using evidence to investigate questions; they *include* cultural relevance when participating in discussions; they *collaborate* in learning communities using a variety of communications tools: They *curate* content for assignments by making critical choices about information sources; they *explore* new perspectives by responding to relevant challenges; and they *engage* with resources and in responsible behavior by evaluating information and how to use it in ethical and legal ways. This framework seeks to encourage the *thinking, creating, sharing,* and *growing* potential of students by acknowledging prior

Figure 4.7. Library Framework

Domains and Competencies		Shared Foundations And Key Commitments					
		Inquire	Include	Collaborate	Curate	Explore	Engage
Domains and Competencies	Think						
	Create						
	Share						
	Grow						

Available at https://standards.aasl.org.

knowledge, encouraging reflection on experience, and fostering ongoing research. This framework represents the thoughtful and effective use of a library, which with the World Wide Web is—everywhere—all of the time. Mr. Lopez's class witnessed their teachers consult resources in real time to solve a real-time problem.

This section of the chapter ends by introducing the Whole School, Whole Community, Whole Child Model, which includes health and physical education and provides an all-encompassing perspective that links with the intellectual tools of the other disciplines. Mr. Lopez and all of the teachers introduced in this chapter engage in transdisciplinary work with their students every day, much of which includes the health indices embedded into this last framework

Model of Health: Whole School, Whole Community, Whole Child

The Centers for Disease Control and Prevention (CDC) has worked with the Association for Supervision and Curriculum Development to prepare the national framework for health education and physical activity for young people, which includes nutrition, school climate, and community (CDC, 2014). This 10-component framework is presented in the Whole School, Whole Community, Whole Child (WSCC) Model, shown in Figure 4.8.

The WSCC model calls for the integration of health services and educational programs. The focus is on keeping young people "healthy, safe, engaged, supported, and challenged." The framework represents the coordination of 10 structures, programs, curricula, policies, services, and practices necessary to ensure healthy, safe, engaging, supportive, and appropriately challenging environments.

The CDC's School Health Index analyzes the ways in which schools promote healthy and safe behaviors among students. Improving student health and safety is associated with:

- Increased students' capacity to learn
- Reduced absenteeism

Figure 4.8. Whole School, Whole Community, Whole Child (WSCC) Model

COMMUNITY ➡	Coordination of Policy, Process, and Practice
Counseling, psychological, and social services	
Nutrition environment and services	
Health education	
Physical education and physical activity	
Social and emotional school climate	
Physical environment	
Health services	
Employee wellness	
Community involvement	
Family engagement	
STUDENTS ➡	Healthy, safe, engaged, supported, challenged

http://www.ascd.org/programs/learning-and-health/wscc-model.aspx.

- Improved physical fitness and mental alertness
- Reduced aggression and violence
- Reduced/prevented alcohol, tobacco, and other drug use
- Reduced punitive disciplinary actions
- Increased academic achievement
- Increased student attachment to school
- Improved social and emotional skills, such as self-regulation, communication, and problem solving (CDC, 2017a, p. 1, 2017b, p. 1)

In a health-threatened, pandemic world, student well-being and safety are even more pronounced and affect every aspect of school life.

EMBEDDING THE "WHAT," GUIDING THE "HOW," PROVIDING A "WHY"

All of the eight frameworks promote education rooted in the notion that learners interpret their experiences and construct knowledge individually, even as they engage with others in multiple forms of interaction. The frameworks enhance each other because they conceptually support each other.

As the classrooms of this chapter have illustrated, the overarching ideas of the frameworks are ways of organizing thinking and behavior. They are transdisciplinary. To illustrate this point, consider one thinking tool, "relationships, structure, and function," in each of the eight national frameworks:

- "Determining how structure and function relate" is one of the seven *crosscutting concepts* of the science framework.
- "Build intentional cross-cultural connections and relationships with others so as to pose and solve problems collaboratively and strengthen independent thought" is one of the six *21st-century literacies* of the language arts framework.
- "Look for and make use of structure" is one of the eight *practices* of the mathematics framework.
- "People create, interact with, and change the structures and functions of power, authority, and governance" is one of the eight *themes* of the social studies framework.
- "Relationships among artistic ideas and works to societal, cultural, and historical contexts" is one of the four *artistic processes* of the core arts framework.
- "Relationship between the products and perspectives of the cultures studied" is one of the five *goals* of the framework for learning languages.
- "Intellectual networks through which one establishes connections with others to build on prior knowledge and create new knowledge" is one cell of the *shared foundations* of the library framework.
- "Health requires coordinating relationships among community structures designed to support families" is one of the 10 *components* of the Whole School, Whole Community, Whole Child Model.

The overlaps are striking. They point to the commonalities that underpin teachers' work across grades and subjects and create a potential through line for the construction of knowledge and skills. Constructivist teachers use the frameworks to "chart the course" of the classroom and engage students in thinking about big, consequential ideas.

PART II: GUIDING PRINCIPLES	
Chapter 4 Tying the Learning Frameworks Together	Students make connections across content, deepen reasoning, and construct transdisciplinary knowledge and skills when teachers use the national frameworks to guide lesson development.
Chapter 5 Framing Curricula and Teaching Around Big Ideas	
Chapter 6 Fostering the Development of Reasoning With Design Thinking	
Chapter 7 Deepening Reasoning With Transdisciplinary Strategies	
Chapter 8 Responsibly Assessing Student Learning	

Framing Curricula and Teaching Around Big Ideas

Teaching that results in enduring learning is a complex endeavor, far more complicated than the transmission of discrete pieces of information from one person to another. This chapter discusses the power of structuring lessons around big ideas, and how these types of lessons pique students' interests and foster meaningful learning.

Teaching with and around and for big ideas is noted in publications across disciplines: big ideas of science (Harlan, 2015), big ideas of math (Toh & Yeo, 2019), big ideas of art (Davis, 2018), and big ideas of social science (Edmonds & Warburton, 2016), to name a few of many.

Here are some examples of big ideas in school subjects:

- "Societies undergo change during times of crisis" in social studies classes.
- "Motion can evoke emotion" in English classes.
- "Algebra relates to structure, relation, and quantity" in math classes.
- "The medium matters" in art classes.
- "Lyrics elevate melody" in music classes.
- "Machines 'think'" in technology classes.
- "We are what we eat" in health classes.
- "Fair play requires an awareness of others" in physical education classes.
- "Multilingualism opens doors" in language classes.
- "Levers make work easier" in science classes.

Most of us learn best whole-to-part, yet most commonly used curricula present ideas part-to-whole. Think of assembling a bookshelf, a classic part-to-whole task. Even here, we rely on the "whole" as a reference. We open the box, take out the parts, and begin reading the directions for assembly. As we follow the written directions and sequentially attach screws and nuts to pieces of the bookshelf, we constantly glance at drawings and photos of the finished bookshelf. Seeing the whole gives context to the parts and directions. Most people need to see the whole in order to make sense of the parts. Big ideas become our frames of reference, and they matter.

Although virtually all syllabi are grounded in big ideas, many present those ideas part-to-whole, breaking big ideas into smaller ones presented to students in a predetermined sequence. This is done under the belief that giving students small parts to master is easier and will eventually enable them to assemble those small parts into larger ideas. Some in fact do, but many don't. Most people need to see the whole in order to make sense of the parts. Thus, constructivist classes typically lead with big ideas designed to generate relevance and interest in finding out more, learning about the parts, and triggering deeper thoughts.

BIG IDEAS AND POINTS OF VIEW

Students think about consequential topics and problems when teachers structure lessons around big ideas, arrange access to appropriate resources, and seek and value students' points of view. Teachers select materials and create contexts for teaching big ideas based on students' ages and experiences and interests, world events, available resources, cultural considerations, geographical realities, and many additional factors that contribute to emerging relevance. They seek to connect students' present points of view with the syllabus material. Let's look into two different settings in which students investigate the same big idea in different ways.

Students Investigate a Big Idea, One Way

Ms. Coronado's class had just finished a physical science unit in which students worked on the big idea: "Levers make work easier." Ms. Coronado taught the science of levers with a variety of resources: playground seesaws, modern industrial cranes, medieval trebuchets, and common kitchen utensils—forks, spoons, and ice tongs. She found out what interested whom. The closer the tie between the big idea and students' personal experiences, the greater the chance of engagement and learning. Many of the students had shown particular interest in catapults of any type, and she decided to capitalize on this interest in the next unit.

The next unit addressed ecology, and Ms. Coronado opened the class with: "Our job is to help transform the vacant lot next door into a landscape of flowers. Let's make catapults to launch native plant seed balls over the fence." As their work proceeded, students asked questions about native plants while they made and tested their mechanical devices. Ms. Coronado used the time to learn about students' current points of view on native plants. What did they know?

   Ms. Coronado's goal was to unfurl students' thinking about the role native plants might play in ecologically restoring an environment. Why native? Why now? Why here? Opportunities to design a catapult connected the two units while tying both academic studies to civic action and environmental stewardship. This opportunity situated their previous learning about levers in a new challenge that involved the ecology of their immediate surroundings.

   Once students are engaged, teachers can extend and broaden lessons to tie students' personal experiences to more novel or targeted contexts. Ms. Coronado started with what students knew and then guided them to what the syllabus wanted them to know.

Students Investigate a Big Idea, Another Way

Let's look at the same big idea of mechanical advantage taught differently. First-grade through 4th-grade students participating in a summer program at a museum of science and engineering spent a week designing their own superheroes and creating extreme, fantastical problems for their superheroes to solve. Students began each day "saving" a well-known superhero from a precarious situation described by their teacher. On this day, Ms. Vivian's students were saving Superman by designing machines to launch the dreaded kryptonite away from him. Prompted by Ms. Vivian, students checked in midway to share their progress and thinking, whether the problem was solved yet or not. Here is a sample of the classroom talk.

- "It wasn't sturdy. So, I put a little stick on the edge and that made it very stable."
- "Mine goes high, but not far. That's what I'm working on now."
- "The kryptonite kept falling off the spoon. I put a brown stick in front of it as a stop. It worked."
- "I had the same problem that Jeremiah had. I got a small cork and taped it onto the spoon."
- "The tape was too strong, so it was almost bending it. I fixed it by taping it on the top instead of the bottom."
- "My problem is similar to Janice's. I got another plate and made the bottom sturdier. I figured the other plate would make the base a little thicker and stronger."

   Statements from this group of elementary school "Superman helpers" provide examples of the research on which Goodman and Martens (2007) report: Open-ended tasks in highly interactive environments encourage student exchange of ideas and prompt students to make connections with prior understandings. Highly interactive environments stimulate both short- and long-term memory, foster active problem solving, and promote deep under-standing of content material (Rushton & Larkin, 2001).

Ms. Coronado and Ms. Vivian both built on their students' interests to uncover points of view on the big ideas of the lesson—what students knew and didn't yet know. The teachers introduced structures and resources to help students reveal their present thinking and form new understandings. Some resources were physical materials for students to use in creating de-vices. Sometimes, the teachers paired students based on similar design prob-lems. At other times, the teachers offered small-group teacher-guided lessons to direct inquiry in more productive ways. At all times, Ms. Coronado and Ms. Vivian negotiated the interplay between and among students and cur-ricula. This approach has been used with thousands of children in hundreds of classrooms with consistent results (Brooks, 2011).

NEGOTIATING CURRICULA

Consider an art teacher offering a lesson on depth and perspective. Ms. Sloane reports that her students' initial attempts to understand and demon-strate these concepts lead to more sophisticated efforts as their experience in creating depth and perspective in an art piece expands. Sometimes Ms. Sloane's negotiations with students result in an immediate "win"—students quickly generate a piece that expresses their understanding. Sometimes there is a "delayed win"—she needs to find new entrances to the concepts, acquire new resources, listen in new ways, reframe the challenge, ask students prob-ing questions, or use different analogies or metaphors or examples. Whether immediate or delayed, the goal is to negotiate a "win."

As Ms. Sloane has discovered, learners often proceed down convention-ally "wrong" paths before finding the "right" ones, creating a winding road rather than a straight line toward the construction of new knowledge. Ms. Sloane seeks and uses students' points of view to steer her teaching as she asks students to apply what they learn from one piece to another. She is constantly determining if her inquiry is appropriate and when and how to shift directions that might lead to more fruitful outcomes. She defines "more fruitful" by the depth of her students' thinking, as demonstrated through their work.

A teacher's capacity to negotiate curriculum with students requires both content knowledge and active listening, as does a teacher's capacity to im-provise—to take journeys away from the specific curriculum but stay within range of the big ideas. There is an element of purposeful improvisation in constructivist classrooms. The ability and willingness of teachers to em-brace improvisation, while it may look unplanned, requires a great deal of preparation, skill and "setting the stage." And, flexibility, too. In planning lessons, constructivist teachers build in opportunities for student questions and comments. Part of the art of teaching is anticipating what some of these questions and comments might be, although certainly not all of them, and viewing them not as interruptions to a lesson's flow but as essential to its flow.

A group of high school students were expressing admiration for their social studies teacher, Mr. Saboe. One student remarked that he pauses a few times during each lesson to ask the students if they have any questions about either the content or the process of the lesson. They often do, and when questions are posed by students the lesson usually veers off in the direction the question necessitates—and then returns to what this student perceives to be the lesson's original intent. When asked why this was important, the student replied, "Because it keeps us with him." Mr. Saboe has a journey in mind and guides the students along the intellectual route. The particular lesson this student described was largely teacher directed but also student informed. On a basic level, Mr. Saboe negotiates curricula and improvises lesson sequence based on student input. He understands that acknowledging students' questions in real time when they are relevant to students helps to "keep them with him." Meaning making requires honoring students' thinking, responding to their confusion, and helping them to transform current conceptions into new ones.

JUST-IN-TIME TEACHING

Let's examine the role of timing in meaning making. Think about measurement, a common academic topic perplexing to many. Throughout the grade levels, teachers struggle with helping students to measure accurately, with appropriate units and labels, in formats suitable to the numbers and context. In elementary school, using a 12-inch ruler to measure a length longer than 12 inches is a dilemma for many students—even though elementary school students have been adding whole numbers greater than 12 accurately on paper for years. In middle school, computing percent increases or decreases that are larger than 100% is mystifying for many—even though students have been successfully multiplying and dividing numbers greater than 100 for years. In high school, articulating that "the mass of an object is a measure of how much matter the object has, and volume is a measure of how much space it takes up" are definitions that elude many students—even though they have been comparing those two values for years as they have successfully calculated density and mass. Students "do" the work—successfully, as defined by their test scores and grades—without always understanding the big ideas that underpin what they do, limiting the transferability of what they have been taught.

Teachers who offer students multiple contextual opportunities to measure, make measuring errors, reflect on and talk about measuring, and debate ways to represent and report measurements increase the likelihood that students will actually understand what their measurements represent and be able to transfer that knowledge to future problems. This is enduring learning.

Constructivist teachers build curricula on the big ideas of the syllabus, then adjust for just-in-time learning opportunities as an outgrowth of what they hear their students say. Think, for example, of a Home & Careers class in which students are baking a dessert. Jane levels off her 2/3 of a cup of sugar and Alivia does not. This is a just-in-time learning opportunity for students when the teacher raises a question about standard measures and the impact those measures have on the product. Think of a 3rd-grade class measuring the classroom's perimeter. One student lines up multiple rulers with no gaps and overlaps. Another student lays the rulers on the floor with no attention to gaps or overlaps. This is a just-in-time learning opportunity for students when the teacher wonders about the differences with students. Teachers who understand the importance of context seize opportunities for learning when they arise.

CONTENT-PROCESS DYNAMIC

Teachers often grapple with the balance between covering curricula and fostering the building of concepts. This content–process dynamic is at play in all classrooms, and it's a delicate dance. Privileging content coverage often creates linear teaching processes that misalign with the experiences and unfolding logic of certain students.

Content and process are not mutually exclusive. Teachers can cover content and foster concept building by soliciting and responding to student questions, statements, or confusions in real time. This spirals concept building around the big ideas of syllabi while simultaneously covering the content and sparking student interest in learning more.

Here are five teachers at different career stages who find personally and professionally fulfilling ways to structure their classrooms around concept building.

Teaching Preschool Scientists

Mr. Rubin leads a group of preschoolers to a small beach nearby the school to collect small stones and abandoned shells. As 4-year-old Mia loads up her bucket with stones, shells, and also water, she notices that one of the shells is upside down and floating while the rest sink to the bottom of the bucket. Excitedly, she shows Mr. Rubin and other classmates who eagerly peer into her bucket. Mr. Rubin promises that they will try to find out more about this curious event the next morning. He asks the children to collect as many different types and sizes of shells as they can before heading back to their classroom. In his mind, Mr. Rubin is adapting tomorrow's curriculum plan to expand on Mia's discovery and the other children's interest.

Mr. Rubin prepares for the next day's investigations of Mia's sinking and floating discovery by setting out the various objects the students collected at the seashore. He fills one big, clear tank and various smaller ones with saltwater and prepares one piece of construction paper for each child. On each paper he has drawn a line down the middle, with a "yes" and "no" at the top of the two columns. To begin the lesson, Mr. Rubin holds up a piece of driftwood and asks: "Do you think that this driftwood will sink? Yes or no?" His intent is to expand on Mia's findings and foster the children's abilities to categorize sinkers and floaters. But Mr. Rubin quickly finds out that the lesson he has planned will require changes.

Will the driftwood sink? James quickly says no, then tentatively puts the driftwood on the paper in the "no" space—while looking at Mr. Rubin, quizzically, as if waiting for confirmation that he is correct. Carter puts his piece of driftwood on the "yes" side of his paper. Mr. Rubin looks at Carter and clarifies, "Oh, you think the driftwood is going to sink." Carter replies enthusiastically "Yes, it's going to float." Carter's placement of the driftwood on the "Yes" side of the paper appears to have been a short version of, "Yes, I think it is going to float," which has the same meaning but is expressed very differently than "No, it is not going to sink," with its double negative construction.

Mr. Rubin listens carefully to James and Carter and concludes that a problem exists. He determines that for his preschoolers there is too much language loading, and the concepts "sink and float" add a new semantic variable (Gleason & Ratner, 2013). When Mia made her discovery the previous day, she never actually used the words "sink" and "float." She just showed her evidence. Perhaps she was saying: "Look, the shell became a boat," and sinking and floating never entered her mind. Mr. Rubin, upon reflection, realizes that maybe his original sink and float categories are not so exclusive, given that a turned-up shell can float and the same one, turned-down, will not. He makes some quick adjustments, and the students begin working on their own sinking and floating piles.

Mr. Rubin's major adjustment was shifting from asking the children to predict where to place the objects on a piece of paper to first testing the objects' behaviors in water themselves. Mr. Rubin came to realize the importance of enabling his students to have firsthand experiences from the beginning. Mia made an important discovery about something that interested her and many of her classmates, and Mr. Rubin now sees a range of more student-centered teaching options he can pursue. He can encourage Mia to show her classmates what she discovered or ask her to replicate it. He could ask if she noticed that the floating shell was turned up. If so, he could ask if the "turned-up/turned-down" position matters, and if it works similarly with all shells. If Mia can't replicate it, he can ask the class to attempt to replicate a floating shell. Or, maybe, the focus on shells is too narrow. Maybe Mia's real surprise was that all of her objects sank, except one. If so, expanding the objects beyond shells might be a learning opportunity.

All teachers in all lessons have opportunities to make decisions about whether and how to adjust. Mr. Rubin now understands that he can change the type of scaffolding he offers the children, and he also knows he needs to keep focused on a big idea. But which big idea? There are many age-appropriate ideas worthy of study in Mia's discovery. What matters in floating and sinking: Is it position, shape, size, color, and so on? And what do these measurement words mean: most, few, many, some, majority, and minority?

Many other questions can emerge as big ideas. Mr. Rubin recognizes that he must select one, even if temporarily, and stick with it, even if temporarily, in order to facilitate a classroom experience targeted toward a learning goal. He decides to ask Mia to tell everyone what she saw and how it surprised her. He then invites the other children to place their objects in the water to see if they sink or float, and if upside-down matters, or not, and proceeds from there. His students learned a lot that day—and so did he. Mr. Rubin's artistry as a teacher was enhanced through this experience.

Teaching Middle School Mathematicians

Most 7th-grade math students learn to measure angles, perimeter, area, surface area, and volume, often in a unit with separate lessons. Students typically solve problems through the application of memorized algorithms and rules.

In Mr. Smith's class, students learn how to make those computations in a unit structured around a painting by the 17th-century Dutch artist, Willem van der Vliet, known for his paintings of scenes and buildings in architectural perspective. Mr. Smith's students learn about the artist's desire to draw the tiled floor of an elaborate building so that it looked "correct." A popular subject of artists' attention in van der Vliet's day was realistically depicting highly admired buildings. Doing so was a valued demonstration of scholarship and artistry. The artist had to be a mathematician as well.

Knowing conventional algorithms and rules is still essential to the work in which Mr. Smith's students are engaged, but they also have an artistic and historical context that engages them. Students in this math class learn to accurately compute area, while also learning the two-point perspective drawing technique employed by artists over centuries to represent width, length, and depth on paper. Mr. Smith introduces students to the work of a renowned artist who used knowledge of angles and perception newly emerging in his day to paint his intended images, and they learn math of geometry and measurement through the quest of an artist (Fitzsimmons, 2007a).

Different from Mr. Rubin, a new teacher who narrowed his focus to one big idea in order to better scaffold students' thinking, Mr. Smith, an experienced teacher, expanded his classroom curriculum by situating it in a historical context illustrating the powerful role of the mathematics of perception in artistic renderings.

Teaching Middle School Historians

What prompted the American Civil War, and what was its impact? These are big questions that are debated among scholars to this day. Mr. Kartal's 8th-grade class is working on several issues embedded in those questions. One group of students focuses on the legal and moral issues involved in one person owning another person; another group studies instances of human activity under state control versus federal control versus any control; another group is interested in the interpersonal dynamics of family members fighting against each other; one group is examining the ties between economics and enslavement; and a fifth group is investigating whether Abraham Lincoln's position on slavery was motivated by conscience, political expediency, or some other reason. Each group huddles, discusses, and engages in its research.

Mr. Kartal is focused on concept building and he invites his students to produce knowledge from information. In concept-building classrooms, social studies students become historians who learn that investigating the history of specific events or situations can shed light on a number of other broad content themes. For example, researching the history of the cotton gin, a mechanical invention that made separating cotton seeds from cotton fiber easier and quicker to do, revealed other complexities to students, such as who really invented the cotton gin: Was it Eli Whitney as most textbooks indicate? Or, was it Kitty Littlefield Greene, the owner of the plantation on which Whitney was working as a tutor, and who, as a woman, was not allowed to file patents? Or, was it Sam and his father, two enslaved workers on the plantation with unknown last names, who also were not permitted to file patents because they had no legal standing? How did the cotton gin affect slavery? What were some of the other social and ethical consequences of the cotton gin? How did it affect economies around the world? These are questions that scholars and historians continue to ask and study. These are questions that history students in concept-building classrooms also ask and study.

Mr. Kartel is a historian. He views his students as historians, and organizes his lessons around large, interesting questions designed to foment uncertainty, generate relevance, and twig interest in knowing more about the topics under study. He asks his students to organize themselves around specific foci within the larger topics, and in so doing they learn not just about the area they are examining, but about the bigger idea, as well.

Teaching High School Biologists

In Ms. Coleman's 9th-grade living environment class, students study cell biology through a publisher's workbook. The students correctly complete questions about the parts of a cell and their functions.

Ms. Coleman's teacher–mentor visits the class and asks students to describe how cells keep organisms alive. Upon listening to their responses, it becomes clear to Ms. Coleman that although students have successfully completed the workbook pages, they understand much less about cell biology than their workbook responses suggest. Students who had accurately labeled the cell membrane as well as the specific layers and channels of the membrane cannot explain its role in the cell's metabolism, and instead default to repeating the labeling on the worksheets. Furthermore, Ms. Coleman is surprised that the students do not seem to understand that the processes happening within and between cells on the microlevel are the same processes happening within and between tissues and organs and systems on the macrolevel.

Ms. Coleman begins discussions with students about their worksheet responses and finds out that her students do not understand the semipermeability of the cell membrane (why and how some materials enter the cell and some exit, but not all). She asks students how the semipermeable nature of the membrane allows the cell to function. Students look quizzically at each other. She suggests that they might want to refer to the diagrams on their worksheets to explain the structures and functions through which cell membranes are semipermeable.

The students assemble in groups around their worksheets and start to talk. One says, "Oh, that's what the protein channels do!" Another says, "I still don't get how some things move out of the cell and others don't." They are now engaged with each other about the puzzle of life they are starting to put together—the topic Ms. Coleman initially thought they understood more clearly. Their comments and questions reveal much about each student's understanding of the topic, more than their worksheet answers indicated.

Ms. Coleman undergoes a major change. She realizes that the successful completion of the assignments isn't necessarily indicative of new learning, and that she must generate greater student-to-student interaction that will allow her to more deeply probe her students' thinking and help her understand what her students know and how she can extend their learning.

As these middle school science students morph into biologists trying to make sense of life, Ms. Coleman vividly witnesses the distinction between covering content and building concepts. Ms. Coleman, a novice teacher, comes to understand that learning parts doesn't always add up to the whole, both in content and pedagogy, and that a straight line isn't always the fastest route for students seeking to build complex concepts. Her active listening helps her better share the wonders of biology with her students.

Process and content are inextricably tied together. Teachers and students "unpacking" content collaboratively is inestimably important. Relying primarily on textbook and workbook assignments, no matter how current or scholarly or aesthetically pleasing those resources may be, often disengages students from pondering big ideas and engages them instead in following directions and part-to-whole learning.

Teaching High School Chemists

Mr. Boro's 11th-grade chemistry class explores a wide array of content, including osmosis, diffusion, molecular size, solubility, oxidation, acidification, composition, among other topics, with questions such as: "What are the benefits of using bronze, compared to other materials, when making a sculpture?" or "How much water is in a handful of popcorn kernels?"

Notice the difference between posing these big-idea questions and requiring students to memorize definitions of osmosis, solubility, and diffusion, which is the more normative assignment in many high school chemistry classes. One approach relies on the traditional method of determining what students have learned: Can they repeat it back to the teacher? The other asks students to apply what they know in responding to more challenging questions.

Students in Mr. Boro's class study interrelationships and make connections between the academic study of chemistry and authentic issues that may affect decisionmaking in their lives. For example, they study the compounds in sodas they frequently drink, the effect of temperature on flavor or the role of heat in cooking, and, in the bronze question above, the process of lost wax casting to make metal sculptures (Fitzsimmons, 2007b).

The popcorn assignment engages students in thinking about measurement of sample sizes and the determination of just how much popcorn is in a "handful," anyway? When the focus is on concept building, students own the questions they seek to answer, they own the process of answering them, and they own the answers.

POSING PROBLEMS OF EMERGING RELEVANCE

The lessons discussed above are designed around big ideas that promote a need-to-know within students and also serve as reflection points for their teachers. The ideas are rooted in questions aligned with the syllabus and are contextualized enough to create some level of emergent relevance—for most of the students—most of the time.

Most elementary students don't wake up in the morning hoping to learn spelling and grammar rules that day. Nor do most middle schoolers leap out of bed excited about learning algebraic equations and algorithms. Not many high schoolers put their heads on their pillows at night anticipating the chance to calculate air speed/air pressure relationships in their physics class the next morning. Most college students aren't titillated by the prospect of writing a thesis on how national identity is expressed through literature for an English course final. Yet, each of these topics, a piece of most academic programs at each of these levels, is important and can become relevant to students. We live in a fascinating and multidimensional world, and schools can be places where that fascination and those dimensions are explored.

Yong Zhao (2018) writes of schools that offer "personalizable education," places that promote students' capacities to organize their own learning. In an earlier work, he writes:

> Only when children learn what they want to learn and begin to take responsibility for learning and living can they stay truly engaged. When they are forced to learn something they don't see as relevant, no matter how important adults believe it will be for their future, children may simply go through the motions at best, and become disengaged and drop out at worst. (Zhao, 2012, p. 171)

Classrooms that invite students to take responsibility for their own learning are rooted in constructivist pedagogy. Ultimately, students create their own relevance. Teachers can't preorganize thinking for students, but they can organize classroom resources in order to maximize the likelihood that students will use them in unique ways geared to tweak their own thinking. Students must have opportunities to select appropriate resources for solving meaningful problems. Materials organization must support the pedagogy.

Think about all the worksheets students are given, with premade tables and graphs to read and interpret, and boxes to fill in. These materials are created by well-intended and highly knowledgeable adults with years of valuable experience, and they make perfect sense to their creators, but they deny students the chance to organize their own thinking. They substitute adult thinking for student thinking. Some teachers view this as modeling how to use graphic organizers, seeing preestablished categories for students as more expeditious than asking them to create categories themselves. Indeed, it does save time, but at a very high opportunity cost. Filling in a blank data table and constructing one's own data table are two very different cognitive tasks. The objective is to have students learn how to create and read data tables in pursuit of making meaning about some issue or phenomenon—not to fill in a data table as an end. This is what creates relevance.

A group of elementary school students is trying to prove or disprove the claim that all metals are attracted to magnets. They begin arbitrarily testing combinations of materials. Mr. Jaheem verbally wonders with one group of students how they will remember what they test and what the results of each test show. He comments, "I wonder if this box could help you keep the piles separated," a statement that guides the students to create a three-dimensional categorization and record-keeping system. Through silently placing materials such as paper and pencil or an iPad within reach, he prompts other students to consider pictorial or graphic forms of record-keeping. Mr. Jaheem makes print and electronic resources available when students perceive them as helpful to the questions under study. The students are creating their own meaningful ways to capture data, which contrasts with filling in blank boxes on a premade data table.

Research shows a difference in achievement between elementary students who use inquiry science kits and those who use everyday materials, design their own experimental approaches, and consult texts as they need them. Students who use their own materials and create their own approaches demonstrate increased achievement, particularly lower socioeconomic students (Slavin et al., 2014). Why? Most kits preorganize activities for students, focusing them on following directions more than inspiring genuine, student-directed investigations. The kits' data charts are premade, ready for filling in. The variables are precontrolled, so as to avoid errors. It's much like following a recipe. The value given to compliance is high, the opportunity to err is diminished, and the chance of important learning is decreased.

Figure 5.1. A Teacher Reflection

I didn't see way back then because I never looked, way back then. My teachers taught me the "1/2 is the inverse of 2" and I verbalized it back, but I didn't really "get" what I was saying. And, I knew I didn't get it. I knew that it didn't really matter to anyone that I really wasn't getting it. My teachers thought that I was a good student. I didn't think I was.

When I began to teach, I revisited the verbalisms. For the most part, I was better able to build some meaning. Sometimes, just maturity allowed ideas to "fall into place." Other times, I struggled to weave the fibers of facts into understandings. I knew I couldn't begin to create curriculum or write lesson plans until I could better understand the topics and concepts in broader contexts and on deeper levels—for myself. So, I made a plan, and it usually worked. I began in the children's section of the library.

That was then. Now I have lots of years of experience—and the Internet. I've relearned, then learned anew most everything I was ever taught, but I still wake up every morning with new questions that I truly can't wait to answer. Yesterday, it was the monarch butterfly migration. How do multiple generations find the same tree 3,000 miles away? And, oh my, are we really losing them all now? The day before it was the song: Auld Lang Syne. Where did that come from?

How have I relearned what I was taught? I search for the big, broad ideas into which smaller, specific ideas fit. This is how I learn, and this is how I invite students to learn.

Slight shifts in classroom environments open spaces for new behaviors. When problems emerge as relevant and the resources for solving those problems are available, students become engaged. All students have endowments and limitations and interact with others everyday along their own individual continua. The key to enabling students' successes is to recognize where they sit along their own continuum of growth and invite activity and discussion that helps each grow from that point. Teaching for big ideas applies to all students.

Let's close this chapter with the reflection of a teacher in Figure 5.1. In order to see, we must look.

PART II: GUIDING PRINCIPLES	
Chapter 4 Tying the Learning Frameworks Together	Students make connections across content, deepen reasoning, and construct transdisciplinary knowledge and skills when teachers use the national frameworks to guide lesson development.
Chapter 5 Framing Curricula and Teaching Around Big Ideas	Students think about consequential topics and problems when teachers structure lessons around big ideas, arrange access to appropriate resources, and seek and value students' points of view.
Chapter 6 Fostering the Development of Reasoning With Design Thinking	
Chapter 7 Deepening Reasoning With Transdisciplinary Strategies	
Chapter 8 Responsibly Assessing Student Learning	

Fostering the Development of Reasoning With Design Thinking

Design thinking is what we bring to problems in need of solutions. Design thinking involves defining problems, caring about what unfolds, and looking for innovative solutions. This chapter offers a close look at how teachers stretch their students' reasoning, creativity, and empathy using curriculum grounded in design challenges, that is, design-based curricular prompts situated in issues important to the worlds in which students live. Solving problems of interest creates learning possibilities and establishes opportunities for broader relevance to emerge.

Design thinking emerged from the field of engineering, became a key problem-solving approach in architecture and business, evolved into its own academic study, and today is a widespread component of many disciplines. Inquiry, creativity, reflection, and experimentation are essential components of most design-thinking models, with obvious connections to constructivist approaches to teaching.

> Design thinking can serve as the missing link between theoretical findings in pedagogy science and the actual practical realisation in schools. It meets the crucial criteria for effective 21st century learning by facilitating interdisciplinary projects, approaching complex phenomena in a holistic constructivist manner. It thereby leads to a transition from the transfer of knowledge to the development of individual potentials. (Rhinow et al., 2012, p. 11)

Emerging research supports this view (Guvenir et al., 2019; Luka, 2014; Scheer et al., 2012).

MODELS OF DESIGN THINKING

Stanford University developed a well-known model for design thinking that is used in many secondary and university programs. It is framed by four rules (Plattner et al., 2016):

- The *human* rule says that all design activity is social in nature.
- The *ambiguity* rule states that uncertainty is inevitable, and experimenting is vital.
- The *redesign* rule reminds us that while technology and social circumstances may change, basic human needs remain constant.
- The *tangibility* rule posits that prototypes make ideas concrete.

Within this framework, design thinking occurs through a five-phase process: Designers initially *empathize* with the people and circumstances of the problem to be solved; *ideate* on solutions by challenging the assumptions thought to be attached to the problem; *define* the needs being addressed by the problem; *prototype* solutions; and finally *test* findings. The cycle repeats itself until a viable solution is generated (Plattner et al., 2016). This is a design cycle. Of note is the model's initial focus on empathy, the abandoning of preconceived ideas of viable solutions and the enlarging of our awareness of other people's needs, perspectives, cultures, or goals.

The Museum of Science in Boston, as part of its *Engineering Is Elementary* program, is well known for its engineering design model used frequently with young children and adolescents. Similar to the Stanford model, it also has five steps: Young designers *ask* questions about the problem to be solved, *imagine* possible solutions, *plan* out the chosen solution, *create* the solution based on the plan, and *improve* the solution based on testing it out (Museum of Science Boston, 2017). The similarities between the two models are highlighted in Figure 6.1.

Design thinking necessarily involves error, which is an essential and unavoidable component of the construction of knowledge. A well-known statement attributed (without verification) to Winston Churchill defines success as the ability to move from failure to failure without the loss of enthusiasm. This is what we hope for in schools. People rarely design precisely what will work on an initial attempt: Engagement in design work embraces error as a necessary step toward success. Students who work on design projects

Figure 6.1. Similarities Between Design-Thinking Models

STANFORD MODEL Often Used in High School and College	BOSTON MUSEUM OF SCIENCE MODEL Often Used in Elementary and Middle School
Empathize	Ask
Ideate	Imagine
Define	Plan
Prototype	Create
Test	Improve

and learn to self-correct based on feedback from their own designs become resilient learners who enjoy school. They learn to fail forward.

FAILING FORWARD

The term "failing forward" was first used in business (Maxwell, 2007) and then popularized within the maker community, a worldwide group of independent innovators who share their inventions at celebrations known as maker faires and collaborate in workshops called makerspaces. The concept of failing forward has relevance here. The term refers to one's capacity to learn from error and see mistakes as important steps toward understanding and accomplishment. It takes away the "right" and "wrong" overlay from works in progress, and the "mis" from misconception. Failing forward views mistakes and errors nonjudgmentally. It is a freeing perspective. The notion is useful for teachers when thinking about how to help students self-correct and appreciate their errors as pathways to success. Failing forward links with the mindfulness attitude of nonjudgment discussed in Chapter 3, and asks: What did I just learn about myself and/or the work in which I'm engaged, and what do I need to change going forward?

When students are not making mistakes, they are likely following directions and/or memorizing. Schools often seek to minimize student error, seeing it as "discouraging" for students. Failing forward classrooms take a different approach. Teachers often report that when they ask students to show and explain their work, many self-correct and say: "Aah, now I see where I went wrong. Thanks." Given a chance to reflect on and explain their thinking, students generally are appreciative of the opportunity to self-assess, generate new, self-determined pathways, and/or better understand teacher-suggested pathways.

When designing within a failing forward mindset, students have the safety to recognize for themselves when and if something isn't working, accept the error or miscalculation as a valued part of the process, and begin reworking the problem with a fresh set of eyes and the capacity to move forward. This is a freedom that opens space for pursuit of deeper meaning and creative expression.

Stornaiuolo and Nichols (2016) report that failing forward is a typically hard concept for students, teachers, parents, and administrators to embrace in schools that are externally designated by authorities as "failing," almost always labeled as such because of low student test scores. Yet, students in schools designated as "failing" are as intellectually curious and creative as students in schools with higher test scores, and they benefit from the same opportunities to fail forward. "Opportunities to fail" has a strange ring to it within the context of schooling—but the benefits of failing forward are undeniable.

INNOVATING WITH DESIGN THINKING

Design thinking is the source of innovation of any type. From the first primitive tools humans fashioned to eat and live to today's advanced forms of artificial intelligence, design thinking has been the springboard. Today's students are as likely to create technology as use it in applications across disciplines. Elementary students work with electronic blocks and cubes to figure out how to wire dollhouses with chandeliers and wall switches. Middle school students illustrate life cycles by superimposing time-stamped computer-generated buds and leaves and other wildlife onto photos of winter landscapes. High school students use the computational thinking of open-source coding languages to learn biology concepts or social studies themes.

Design thinking can and does occur anywhere, but schools that intentionally create curricular spaces and/or build physical spaces for collaborative design thinking report greater student and teacher engagement in the process (Counsell et al., 2015; Nair, 2014). Perhaps one of the most visible ways to appreciate the energy generated through design thinking is to consider the number of new makerspaces popping up with increasing frequency in libraries, universities, community centers, and schools (Herold, 2016).

Learning Spaces as Makerspaces

Makerspaces are usually labs, studios, or work areas that provide the physical space, materials, equipment, and teacher support for inventive design thinking, reflection, and action. There are all types of makerspaces.

Community and university versions with specialized equipment and supplies serve, for example, fiber art study groups, yarn bombers (knitters who "blanket" unlikely items, such as trees), quilters, wood sculptors, or gaming programmers. There are makerspaces in schools in which students learn to design code in user-friendly, visual languages and incorporate microcontrollers into a wide range of projects: Students create animated videos of political boundaries in geography lessons, interactive paintings or instruments in art or music classes, or virtual games that simulate economic policies in social studies lessons. In schools without dedicated areas, makerspaces are set up in the school library or cafetorium for specified periods of time, offering students opportunities to work on projects using a variety of resources, from specialized electronic building blocks to everyday materials such as foam board, tape, and used mailing boxes. Some teachers have created makerspace corners in their own classrooms. Some teachers have turned their whole classrooms into makerspaces. Makerspaces are learning spaces.

Irrespective of what the space looks like or where it is situated, the purpose is to provide opportunities for students to reflect on and engage in design, often with each other, sometimes by themselves. Design plays a vital role in the construction of knowledge. It is becoming ever more common and is integrated into literacy.

Coding as Problem Solving, Coding as Literacy

Seymour Papert, in his groundbreaking work, *Mindstorms: Children, Computers and Powerful Ideas* (1980), suggested that learning to code is learning how to find and fix problems that are bound to occur. As they develop, before learning to code, young children learn to speak by using the units of language of their environment—in accord with the rules of that language. They may say that they sang yesterday and, then in accord with the rules they infer, they often say that they "brang" home the song they sang. As they mature, they learn to "fix" that logical "error," and say that they "brought" it home.

Coding a computer to perform a task is similar. It is the process of creating a set of instructions in a language and with the logic the computer understands. Anyone can learn to code without a computer because the logical set of instructions to perform a task can be created on paper or in other media. Papert was a leader in recognizing the learning potential of computers in education. He developed Logo, the first programming language for children. He considered learning at one's leading edge to be the process of engaging in activities in which one does not know initially what to do or how to do it. Students build knowledge and then rebuild as they encounter new information and attempt to make sense of it. He heralded the notion that children learn *by* programming computers and cautioned against adults trying to use computers *to* program children.

Today's literacy includes coding, and the logic of coding begins with design thinking. Returning to the Stanford model, learning how to code includes learning about oneself and others (empathizing, ideating, and defining) and getting unstuck from problems (prototyping and testing). Douglas Rushkoff, a media theorist known for coining the term *"digital native,"* comments that all students need some exposure to coding because citizenry in a world filled with computers demands it:

> Our kids aren't Facebook's customers; they're the product. The real customers are the advertisers and market researchers paying for their attention and user data. But it's difficult for them or us to see any of this and respond appropriately if we don't know anything about the digital environment in which all this is taking place. (Rushkoff, 2012, para. 2)

Rushkoff sees coding literacy as a critical element in a digital world. Just as learning to read includes learning to write and learning to listen includes learning to speak, learning to use computers must include some level of learning to program them. Coding is thinking. It is breaking big ideas into smaller ones and putting small pieces back together to make big ones.

Many tend to think of coding as complex, sophisticated work most suitable for mature thinkers. However, young children can begin to learn to code by thinking about the logic of making something as simple as mud pies. They *proceed in steps* (I get a bucket, then some dirt, then some water), and a teacher can help them begin to recognize that they are engaging in steps; they occasionally *repeat steps* (I get more water); they know that sometimes the *steps can only occur under certain circumstances* (when it's recess); they know that sometimes *something happens that interferes* with the process (it's thundering and the teacher calls us in early); they know that sometimes lots of things happen and *another tool is needed*, maybe a tray (Emma wants me to carry her sweater back to class and I want to carry my plate of mud pie and water bottle and I only have two hands), and so on. Mud pie making may not look like coding, but young mud pie makers can begin to learn the power of sequencing, repeating, changing conditions, surprises, and collecting more material when interacting with a teacher who recognizes that these factors describe how basic coding occurs and helps to narrate the process for them.

Describing how to make a mud pie illustrates common programming commands:

- *Sequence* (get materials)
- *Iteration* (get additional materials)
- *Conditional statements* (only if it's recess)
- *Variables* (oh no, it's thundering)
- *Arrays* (needing a tray for all this stuff)

These programming commands form the basis of coding. As young programmers mature, teachers can engage them in more sophisticated tasks, and their capacities to program those tasks grow in sophistication, as well. The making of an app to address the interest of a classmate, for instance, is an example of programming that involves more sophisticated logic. There are countless apps developed by students: One example is a student who developed an app that advises users on how to dress for the predicted weather, which is now available for sale at a well-known online store.

Eyes on Parity

Some significant historical disparities are connected to design thinking. Gender inequality is one. Coding has traditionally been a male-dominated enterprise. Statistics on makerspaces also reveal a significant disparity in gender engagement: Participation has historically been male. Hour of Code is a worldwide effort to expose students to the logic and creativity of coding, particularly women and minorities underrepresented in the computer science field. Hour of Code uses self-guided activities involving logic but not necessarily requiring computers. One hundred million students have participated. Whereas participation of female students in computer science studies or workforce is 20%–25%, female participation in Hour of Code is 50%.

Vossoughi et al. (2016) call for attention to sociopolitical and socioeconomic variables as "making" is being adopted in schools, and argue that equity and access across gender, ethnicity, culture, race, and orientation must be considered and proactively fostered. Today's students are today's and tomorrow's producers of continually expanding technologies capable of solving societal problems. Parity is paramount. Schools are paying attention.

The opportunities within makerspaces and the concept of failing forward often include technology of some type, electronic or nonelectronic. Together or alone, everyone is working with or on something to make sense of something. When inspiration arises, even theoretical physicists need a pencil and the back of an envelope!

DESIGN CHALLENGES

Design challenges are problems that require design thinking in order to generate possible solutions. They take many forms. Under a broad definition, a design challenge may be designing an argument for determining what medical supplies should be sent to a hospital in a remote community; or designing a system for selecting recycled tiles for the lobby of a new school; or designing a device for rescuing a person trapped in the aftermath of an earthquake.

Effective design challenges invite the integration of creative and critical thinking through the design process. Teachers set up model scenarios with problems to solve and serve as master learners as they interact with students around novel situations (Brooks & Caliendo, 2012). For example, in the case of the rescue challenge, the person is a doll, the crevice of the fallen structure is the space under a classroom chair, and the fifth floor of a building is a classroom bookshelf. In creating solutions, students research, read, write, listen, speak, plan, measure, compute, collaborate, and learn from one another. With teacher support, students find approaches and related resources that inform next steps and bring them closer to desired solutions. Through careful observation, teachers offer appropriately challenging questions, not difficult enough to provoke frustration or anxiety, and not easy enough to evoke dismissive attitudes.

Design challenges are intentionally planned classroom scenarios that teachers introduce to stimulate and extend students' purposeful thinking. A teacher's goal in presenting design challenges is to stimulate cognitive churn and capture students' attention. Teachers then adjust the challenges with new materials, media, specimens, books, or questions. Often, teachers plan for challenges using community resources such as data sets, political polls, or local surveys. Book passages, video segments, photos, and articles, all accompanied by a targeted question or task, promote the development of reasoning skills, relevant vocabulary, and task commitment.

Teachers often create design challenges by using commonly found resources from the manufactured or natural world, such as kitchen powders or solutions that behave in unpredicted ways or seed pods that twirl in unanticipated patterns when falling or garage tools used for art making. Two materials that surface again and again as fundamental substances that help students better understand their worlds across disciplines are water and salt. There is much to learn from these two basic resources. The more we know about water and salt, the more we understand global economics (read *Salt: A World History* by Mark Kurlansky), art and culture (ever try the Ebru tradition of marbling paper to achieve swirls of colorful curves?), math (what do you know about the substance on which the metric system is based?), ecology and health (why are estuaries so important?), and so many other domains. Salt and water are examples of the wide range of everyday materials with which teachers can create accessible, meaningful challenges.

There are design challenges within all subject disciplines. Design thinking can be applied in any subject and is not limited to challenges requiring a physical product or service. In one high school class, students debate whether philanthropists who give huge sums of money to improve education should enjoy an outsized say over education policies and the future direction of American schools. Students on both sides of the issue design an argument. They consult newspaper editorials and columns with different perspectives on the matter, and then share their points of view. As the discussion progresses, some students' initial positions harden while other students' views change. In this discussion, student thinking ranges from "Yes, money talks" to "It's a moot point because education shouldn't accept any private funding" to "No, if education accepts private funding, those giving money shouldn't have more say than anyone else." Students listen to their peers, try to empathize with their points of view, and *design* and *redesign* arguments that respond to the flow of the conversation. Students are engaging in design thinking to solve a design challenge.

Although students will not all create the same knowledge through design challenges, they will create knowledge new to them while either reinforcing or challenging their prior thinking. When students are designing solutions, they are building ideas—writing an argument that forwards a position they hold, applying a math algorithm that renders a quantity, engaging in an experimental method that produces a finding, drawing a model that creates a new space or product, composing a song that shares a feeling, organizing a rally that deepens awareness of an issue: These are just some of the countless academic tasks that engage students fully. In these classrooms, there are always new ideas to investigate because the solution to one design challenge inevitably leads to another.

TEACHING WITH DESIGN CHALLENGES

Students in Ms. Contreras's middle school technology class are studying forces by building cars and ramps. The design challenge is to create a car and a ramp system for a driver with mobility limitations. The aim is for the car, when released from the top of the ramp, to stop 7 feet from the end of the ramp, just at the spot where the driver's wheelchair sits. Some students first focus on particular aspects of the car (its wheels, the length of its body, its height off the ground, etc.); others focus initially on the ramp (its angle off the floor, its height, whether there is a point at which it could be too steep and impede the car's movement when it hits the ground, etc.); and still others look first at the materials to determine matches between the cars and ramps (what would be too much friction, what might be too little, what role will weight play).

Students' work remains speculative until their first trials. Once they see for themselves how their car/ramp system functions, each group makes modifications with the driver's safety in mind. As Ms. Contreras listens to students' discussions, she introduces vocabulary that reflects their work and poses questions that encourage students to consider speed, direction, angles, mass, friction, and acceleration. She uses these terms carefully and scaffolds her students' precise use of the terms. Students learn to speak with classmates about analysis, prediction, and logic, among other cognitive concepts, and also learn to deal with uncertainty and ambiguity. Their initial "errors" lead them to improvements with each new iteration.

When offering feedback, Ms. Contreras is equally precise because language precision extends learning. Does a student's work "use novel materials" or "make a compelling case for a low center of gravity," or "emerge from analysis of data?" There are countless examples of meaningful ways to communicate with students that go beyond "excellent," "good work," and "fine job." Ms. Contreras uses terminology that helps students pinpoint what is "good" about their work themselves, without relying on her external validation.

Figure 6.2 provides a framework for teachers to think about their work in real time while providing design challenge lessons.

Civic Engagement and Career Awareness

Design challenges linked to potential careers and civic engagement spark student involvement because they relate directly to issues that affect students' daily and future lives. Including potential careers in design tasks can

Figure 6.2. Design Challenge Implementation

What to Do	Why to Do It
Introduce challenge and anticipate basic materials.	Challenges invite design thinking. Design thinking supports skill development and a fail forward mentality. Fail forward thinking establishes self-agency and initiative.
Encourage students to try out their ideas.	Even if it is likely that student ideas will not work, providing students the opportunity to "fail" under controlled conditions develops intellectual and emotional stamina. Ideas that "work" after perseverance develop trust in one's efficacy and help students understand that error is an indispensable aspect of learning.
Carefully observe students' actions, expressions, and statements.	Intentional observation and active listening open windows into student reasoning, which allows for more targeted questions, comments, and interventions, and helps students move to their next levels of thinking.
Determine interventions and pose contradictions.	Targeted interventions foster students' pattern seeking and increased awareness of outcomes. Posing contradictions invites students to think about their ideas in new ways, even when their ideas are "right."
Intervene with questions and comments, not judgment.	Teacher responses either promote or impede student thinking and activity. Withholding judgmental responses and offering descriptive feedback encourages students to continue exploring ideas.
Suggest diverse modalities for representing learning.	Diverse representations, such as photography, diagrams, pictures, poems, sentences, discussion, measurements, podcasts, and video support can extend students' communication skills and spark interest in developing new ones.

expand students' conceptions of possibilities for personal fulfillment and rewarding work. Students can learn to be protectors of human rights or the environment, or advocates for issues important to them, or players in all types of causes that are personally, locally, nationally, and/or internationally meaningful—and also meaningful to people they care about and respect.

Consider the following challenge:

- You've been hired as a material engineer to design a travel mug for photojournalists assigned to the Arctic. Design a mug that will keep your water sample at a constant temperature. Create an advertisement for your creation.

The teacher and students discuss the role, needs, and contributions of photojournalists; the geography and climate of the Arctic and the travel required to get there; the value, costs, and potential benefits of Arctic research; and the power of communication, among a variety of other issues. This challenge cuts across many disciplines.

The following design challenges, although situated in specific subjects, also engage students in interdisciplinary study.

- In a high school English or social studies class: You are a novelist creating a fictional story about a Palestinian and an Israeli leader attempting to work collaboratively on a secret plan for peace: Who are they, how did they come together, where do they meet, what is their proposal, and what obstacles will they confront?
- In a middle school math class: You are a graphic artist. The values of the tiles are as follows: yellow = 1, red = ½, blue = ⅓, and green = ⅙. Using the tiles and their assigned values, create a picture with a value of 9⅓. Transform your picture into a piece of kinetic art.
- In an elementary school social studies class: You are a community organizer designing drop boxes for the Red Cross. Construct a package that will protect 12 grams of perishable food when dropped from a height of 1 meter. How about adding a light to increase the visibility of the package at night?
- In a primary school geography class: You are a civil engineer studying the mechanics of sand. Create a sand–water formula that can build a sturdy sandcastle at least 12 inches high.

Teachers who link learning activities with selected jobs expose students to occupations never before known to them: landscape architect, consumer advocate, community organizer, museum curator, art conservator, laboratory technician, medical illustrator, hydrologist, cartographer, artificial intelligence programmer, laboratory technician, and a host of others. In tackling design challenges, students witness a wider field in which to pursue potential dreams. Youth identity is a predictor of future career choices and influences how students conduct themselves in various classes (Tai et al., 2006). Students see new possibilities and walk into classes wondering: "Who am I going to be today?"

Teachers who include the backgrounds, professions, and occupations of students' families deepen engagement and open doors to community involvement. One student made a video for her science class interviewing her mother, a hairstylist, about airflow and evaporation as related to hair dryers. Seeing the science embedded in hair styling enabled the students to think about how science is embedded in so many other everyday activities. Bringing the community into the science classroom brings science to the community.

A Sense of Belonging

Engagement generates a sense of belonging. Students have a commitment not only to the work they are doing, but also to the people with whom they are doing it and the setting in which the work is occurring.

In a university-based teaching laboratory serving teachers and students from an alternative high school, student engagement in tasks, student acceptance of error as part of the process, and student voice in identifying and structuring their own learning activities drove higher attendance rates (Caliendo & Brooks, 2013). The program was a yearlong class based on constructivist pedagogy. Students selected the materials they thought appropriate for the design challenges and the formats through which they demonstrated their learning. The class met 2 days per week, 3 hours per day, to work on STEAM design challenges. Many of the students in this program had repeated 1 to 3 years of high school due to truancy and the concomitant lack of credits toward graduation. For these students, the average school attendance rate at the beginning of the year was approximately 20%. By midyear, school attendance on university program days ranged from 93% to 100%. Periodically, some of the high school students would show up, unscheduled, on a day in which the lab was being used by elementary school programs. Upon arrival, they asked: "What are these little kids doing in our class?" They experienced a sense of belonging and were concerned that others were in their space.

The classes that participated in the teaching laboratory had a number of English language learners and also a number of special needs learners, all of whom were unrecognizable to casual visitors to the lab. Instructors used a range of carefully selected materials, engaged in active listening, and asked deliberate questions. Classmates served as translators when necessary. Design challenges provide a strong foundation on which language and literacy skills, self-regulation, and self-confidence develop.

Through another program in the laboratory serving younger students, dozens of elementary teachers reported that their young English language learners routinely participated in the lab's design challenges with more frequency and enthusiasm than they did in more traditional lessons at school. The laboratory's master teacher noted increased student risk taking in problem solving and heightened capacity to initiate ideas and self-correct. Analyses of student survey data and students' written reports indicated increased career awareness and a marveling at career possibilities (Caliendo & Brooks, 2013).

Design challenges structured around large, consequential ideas that enable students to engage fully are appropriate for all students. All students think, wonder, and question, and all can benefit from the opportunity to do so collaboratively with their classmates.

Many students look to their teachers for clarity and certainty, but not everything is clear; all questions don't have only one right answer; and there are often many shades of gray surrounding issues. To a large degree, it is the valuable struggle with ambiguity that enables students to remain engaged and construct meaning. Voltaire wrote in 1770, "Doubt is not a pleasant condition, but certainty is an absurd one" (Radcliffe, 2017). When students are cognitively confused or when they reach different conclusions than others, a teachable moment has arisen.

Sometimes spontaneous surprises not intentionally planned by the teacher arise, such as encounters with unexpected phenomena or perceived discrepancies or oddly behaving materials or—a spider found in the classroom. They become opportunities teachers can use. In these situations, teachers, as master learners, co-investigate these puzzlements with students, creating, over time, a culture of curiosity in the classroom. Puzzlements cause cognitive confusion. Acknowledging and addressing confusion results in intellectual growth.

Teachers who understand design thinking and incorporate design challenges, plan for provocations, and embrace puzzlements keep their own minds active as master learners and keep their students focused on solving a problem, meeting a need, or working through a conundrum. They are opening students' minds and helping students sense the comfort, purpose, and responsibility of belonging.

PART II: GUIDING PRINCIPLES	
Chapter 4 Tying the Learning Frameworks Together	Students make connections across content, deepen reasoning, and construct transdisciplinary knowledge and skills when teachers use the national frameworks to guide lesson development.
Chapter 5 Framing Curricula and Teaching Around Big Ideas	Students think about consequential topics and problems when teachers structure lessons around big ideas, arrange access to appropriate resources, and seek and value students' points of view.
Chapter 6 Fostering the Development of Reasoning With Design Thinking	Students stretch their understanding, creativity, empathy, and resilience with error when teachers engage them in and scaffold authentic design challenges.
Chapter 7 Deepening Reasoning With Transdisciplinary Strategies	
Chapter 8 Responsibly Assessing Student Learning	

Deepening Reasoning With Transdisciplinary Strategies

The classrooms presented in previous chapters illustrate teachers engaging students with big ideas by offering relevant challenge-based curricula and honoring students' points of view. This chapter amplifies those images with 12 specific transdisciplinary strategies that teachers can adapt for specific settings, subjects, grades, and student needs. These strategies, supported by the science of learning, require the artistry of the teacher for their effective expression. See Figure 7.1.

Students take cues from their teachers. Teachers who are reflective about their work model reflectiveness for their students. Teachers interested in their own continuous improvement model intellectual growth for their students. Teachers with genuine passion for the content they teach help their students to engage with interest and see relevance. And teachers who seek and value students' points of view help students to understand that their thinking matters, that the thinking of their classmates matters, and that there are multiple ways to look at complex issues.

When schools offer only conventional narratives that are different from students' real-life understandings, without seeking to uncover what their

Figure 7.1. Transdisciplinary Strategies

1. Ordering learning experiences
2. Hearing the questions students hear
3. Offering time to think
4. Seeking elaboration
5. Facilitating the search for patterns
6. Valuing evidence
7. Connecting students to each other
8. Posing targeted questions
9. Appreciating context
10. Cultivating a sense of place
11. Supporting student agency
12. Navigating error

students already know or believe to be true, opportunities for learning are frequently muted. Teaching that leads to enduring learning always seeks students' points of view. For example, elementary students often are told that mixing all the colors of light makes white—while every elementary student "knows" that mixing all colors makes brown. They know it so well that they don't hear all colors *of light* make white light. Middle school students are taught that a feather and a bowling ball will fall at the same rate in a vacuum, while every middle schooler knows the bowling ball will get to the ground first. They know it so well that they don't hear that the feather and the bowling ball are falling *in a vacuum*. And high school students are taught that "all men are created equal," while every high schooler knows from personal experience and watching the news that all *people* are not *treated equally, either by their fellow citizens or in the eyes of the law.*

When schools try to "give away" knowledge that doesn't fit with what students know, students either become confused and ask questions to resolve the disequilibrium or they accept that colors in school combine to white, memorizing what they are told even though they know that in the world in which they live combining all the colors in their paint set actually produces brown. To a large extent, when the latter occurs, students come to understand that there is "school stuff" and there is "real life stuff," and they simply stop trying to make sense out of "school stuff."

The following teaching strategies help students make sense of what they are being taught in school.

1. ORDERING LEARNING EXPERIENCES

Ordering learning experiences matters. How teachers sequence lessons is a function of the interplay between curricular knowledge—*what* is being studied—and pedagogical knowledge—*how* students learn.

In a 3rd-grade class, children watch their teacher mold three buckets of clay into eight balls each and give one ball to each of the 24 children in the class. The students count the 24 balls in unison and shake their heads "yes" when asked if each child got a "fair" share. Each child has one. One what? One ball of clay? One-eighth of a bucket of clay? One-twenty-fourth of the total clay? All of these statements are true. Each clay ball is 1, 1/8, and 1/24, simultaneously, dependent on the context and rest of the sentence. For students just beginning to construct understandings of fractions, that's a puzzlement. Did the students consider the ball of clay 1/8 of one total and simultaneously 1/24 of another total? The students acknowledged that they received a "fair share" of clay. To know how to proceed, the teacher needs to know what "fair" means to them.

Most math curricula seek to develop students' capacities to compute with unit fractions (fractions that have one as the numerator) as a component of flexible understanding of whole numbers that share the same principles. Did the students know that, when the teacher divided the clay, they were witnessing a demonstration of the relativity of fractions? They saw something happen. But, what did they see? What sense did they make from what they saw? Piaget's work tells us that children's thinking can put them worlds apart from adult thinking, even if all are in the same room witnessing the same event. Similarly, in discussing how children come to understand number, Papert (1980) writes:

> Children don't conceive number, they make it. And they don't make it all at once or out of nothing. There is a long process of building intellectual structures that change and interact and combine. (p. 4)

Fosnot and Dolk (2001) describe the teaching of mathematics as supporting children's journey along the landscape of learning toward the horizon, with strategies, big ideas, and cognitively accessible models being the focal points of teacher scaffolding. In the case above, shifting from the teacher demonstrating the decomposing of buckets of clay to inviting students to decompose their own buckets of clay, and trying to name the fractional pieces of clay from the whole quantity, might begin to enable students to build the intellectual structures necessary to compare fractions. This one shift in sequence alone invites students into numerical thinking.

Sequence is a critical consideration. Traditionally, lessons are structured sequentially in three phases—concept introduction, concept application and, if time exists, concept exploration. The learning cycle model (Atkin & Karplus, 1962; Lawson & Karplus, 2002) suggests that learning is enhanced when concept exploration precedes concept introduction, which would then be followed by concept application through which the concept is transferred to or investigated in a new context. Rather than introduce–apply–explore, the learning cycle suggests that explore–introduce–apply fosters greater concept building and deeper understanding. See Figure 7.2.

It is through this sequence that students experiment with materials and explore ideas as a precursor to the more formal introduction of concepts, after which they apply what they have learned to new situations. In the concept exploration phase, students "play around" with ideas, investigate materials, examine raw data, gather evidence relating to the topic being studied, and articulate their puzzlements or disequilibrium *before* they read or hear

Figure 7.2. Comparison of Lesson Sequences

Traditional Lesson Sequence	Learning Cycle Sequence
Concept introduction	Concept exploration
Concept application	Concept introduction
Concept exploration	Concept application

the expert views. This generates understandings and questions that make the formal introduction of the topic more attainable. Students' points of view guide the teacher's formal introduction. During the concept introduction phase, students typically read relevant texts and listen to explanations of the topics by their teachers or other experts. They align or juxtapose what they are learning with the initial conceptions they formed during exploration, and either reinforce or modify their thinking. In the concept application phase, they then apply their learning in a more structured assignment situated in a new context.

The learning cycle also addresses the inequity that so often exists in classrooms in which certain students have more background experiences relevant to the curriculum than others. This approach takes nothing away from students who may have had broader backgrounds. The exploration phase provides all students with equal opportunities to consolidate ideas through working with materials or revisiting materials in a new way, while the teacher observes and plans for differentiation within the concept introduction phase. For students with less background in the topic, the exploration phase provides a platform of experience to which students can refer in concept introduction lessons and from which they can explore what comes next.

The learning cycle model also informs how teachers introduce vocabulary. A common practice is "preteaching" difficult vocabulary, buttressed by the belief that it makes new words found in texts easier to understand. Constructivist teachers think differently about this type of practice. Rather than preteaching vocabulary, they typically do the opposite, introducing new vocabulary to students only when new words or terms serve as useful shorthand for students' expression of their thinking, when the new vocabulary is needed to make conversation more efficient or understandable. Think back to how Ms. Contreras introduced new vocabulary in her car/ramp lesson described in Chapter 6. Teachers can introduce "revolution," for instance, after hearing students talk about "things going around and around something else," and they can introduce "rotation" when students refer to something "spinning or twirling" or "like a ballerina."

Offering opportunities for students to play with ideas before introducing text or offering explanations with conventional vocabulary allows students to focus on meaning making. These opportunities trigger activation of the recognition, strategic, and affective networks of the brain, as discussed in Chapter 3, through multiple forms of representation, expression, and problem-based engagement.

2. HEARING THE QUESTIONS STUDENTS HEAR

Hearing the questions students hear matters. Teaching for meaning depends on hearing what students say, which reflects what they think at the time.

Teachers who uncover students' thinking are positioned to help them construct more advanced understandings critical to their ongoing cognitive growth. This is true for teachers of students across ages and subjects.

Piaget famously said that children usually answer correctly the questions they pose to themselves. Those questions are not always aligned with the questions their teachers pose. It is often the case that students hear different questions because of how they interpret them.

Students don't always hear the same questions teachers believe they ask. For example, in a middle school English class discussion about the book *Where the Red Fern Grows* (Rawls, 1961), the teacher asks her students if freeing the Ghost raccoon and fighting the mountain lion had been worth the cost of Billy losing his two dogs. A few students harken back to the money Billy saved to purchase Old Dan and Little Ann, perceiving the word "cost" in the question as referring to his financial investment. Upon hearing their responses, the teacher validates that there were financial costs to buying the dogs and reframes her question by asking if there are additional emotional costs in losing them. That acknowledgment and clarification enabled those students to make sense of the question and engage in the discussion.

Meaningful communication rests on understanding. In this example, the teacher uncovers the students' meaning and reframes the question. When confronted with unexpected student responses that are difficult to analyze, asking "Can you tell me what question you are answering?" usually continues the discussion with fuller engagement by all. On a broader level, these types of questions give every student voice and elevate the cultural responsiveness of the classroom community. Each student's cultural background is an asset. Offering students opportunities to reveal their perspectives develops their skills in making connections between what they already know and what they are learning.

3. OFFERING TIME TO THINK

Offering students time to think matters. For students to be critical and creative thinkers, they need both the opportunities to engage in work that promotes thinking and the time to think. Students need sufficient time to ponder questions and formulate responses. When teachers call on quick-responding students, acknowledge the right answer, and move on to the next question, many students are left behind, perhaps still curious about the previous question but now trying to refocus their attention on the next one. Typically, a not-so-subtle competition develops. The more quickly students can get their hands in the air, the more likely they will be recognized by the teacher. In these fast-paced, rapid response settings with convergent questions, quickly accepting "right" answers actually interferes with thinking and learning. Many students conclude that there is no point in engaging because by the time they are ready to share their thinking, the question will have been answered by someone else and the moment is gone. Some simply shut down.

For several reasons, teachers often offer answers and explanations before their students have had time to explore ideas independently and generate their own questions and responses. First, many teachers see time as scarce, which creates tension to "cover" the syllabus. Sharing their content expertise with students through straightforward demonstrations and direct explanations permits them to move units along expeditiously. A second reason relates to the impatience and expectations of students themselves and the pressure teachers feel to respond to those expectations. Some students, especially those who excel at memorization and enjoy the success of high marks on tests, simply don't want to "waste" time thinking. They just want their teachers to tell them what they need to know, memorize it, and move on. And, third, for some teachers, particularly at the secondary level, being the primary source of information comports with their personal image of teaching. It is how they were taught and how school always has worked for them.

Every student thinks in a different way and at a different pace. Simple structural shifts, such as asking students to ponder questions in dyads or triads, prompts greater numbers of students to engage and enables the teacher to differentiate follow-up questions and modify assignments.

4. SEEKING ELABORATION

Seeking elaboration matters. It is common to misread what students know by accepting initial responses without seeking further elaboration, and it is easy to assume that students' responses reveal targeted knowledge and understandings, especially if responses match teacher expectations. But students may be thinking very differently than what the teacher assumes. It is the elaboration of one's initial ideas that reveals what one knows and understands.

Think of the high school guidance counselor meeting with a senior about his college preferences. The student reveals the name of a well-regarded college for which he would be a perfectly viable applicant. The counselor says, "Okay, good choice." That's a validating response that is likely to please the student. But what if the counselor instead asks, "Does it offer the clubs and activities in which you've participated in high school? Does the school's program offer classes aligned with the climate science studies in which you are so interested?" The guidance counselor is encouraging the student to explain what he knows about the school and how it aligns with his interests. Seeking elaboration is a practice that can prompt students to become increasingly metacognitive. It reveals assumptions and suppositions that cause students to question their current thinking.

The wonderment of Emma, a 2nd-grade student, provides another example: "I wonder, if you drink alcohol before you go out at night, would mosquito bites still itch?" (Brooks, 2002, p. 18). That question could easily have been dismissed as odd, but the teacher's request for elaboration revealed that earlier in the year Emma had learned that when mosquitoes bite people they inject saliva to thin the blood (it serves as an anticoagulant), and it is the saliva that causes the bite to swell and itch. In that day's health class, Emma learned that drinking alcohol thins the blood. So, she conjectured that if a person's blood is already thinned by drinking alcohol, maybe the mosquito wouldn't have to inject its saliva, and the bite would itch less. She connected dots that made perfect sense to her. All students, irrespective of grade level and age, have similar thinking about phenomena they experience. They are always connecting dots—sometimes accurately, sometimes not. We only know their thinking when we open space for it by asking for elaboration.

Posing contradictions is one form of elaboration that can generate productive cognitive disequilibrium. When students are studying complex issues such as "climate change," posing contradictions to those who think that humans have contributed to this change and those who think the opposite requires both groups of students to consider more variables, look for more information, and construct an argument or line of reasoning that directly addresses the contradiction. This process initially challenges certainty and then leads to more refined understandings. Whether students are "right" or "wrong" in their initial responses to questions, asking for elaboration provokes students to rethink both the answer and the process of formulating it.

5. FACILITATING THE SEARCH FOR PATTERNS

Facilitating the search for patterns matters. Much of the research of the developmentalists described in Chapter 3 highlights pattern recognition for its role in cognitive development, and many of the frameworks of the learning standards described in Chapter 4 value it as essential to promote learning. For these reasons, explicitly fostering students' search for and noticing of patterns merits inclusion in this list of teaching strategies.

Two common examples of simple patterns are skip counting and color sequences and the capacity to predict which number or color will come next. A more sophisticated example of pattern recognition is determining where in the sky to look for a rainbow after days of showers followed by sun. At all grade levels, teachers prompt students to use what they know from one domain to explore new domains. Doing so prompts students to see patterns across subjects—to use ideas from geometry in writing poetry, ideas from engineering in explaining how the human skeleton works, or knowledge of Latin in predicting a plant's structure based on its name.

A quote attributed to the composer Claude Debussy reminds teachers of the transdisciplinary nature of life experiences and also school curricula: "Music is the arithmetic of sound as optics is the geometry of light" (quoted in Simonton, 1994, p. 110). The mathematics, science, and artistry of music is a sophisticated system of simple ideas: long and short, loud and soft, quick and slow. These are "little words" for big ideas. The concept of size, or magnitude, is a big idea. Students who seek patterns among the magnitude of an object or phenomenon and its behaviors or characteristics embark on intellectual journeys that open up new ways of thinking.

The teachers introduced in earlier chapters incorporate pattern seeking into their lessons. In Chapter 2, Ms. Adisa invites students to look for patterns in their natural environment. Mr. Tan asks students to discern patterns in how oil in water affects wildlife. Ms. Goodwell invites her students to look for patterns involving human activity and climate change. Ms. Dale and Ms. Chang challenge their students to recognize patterns in how human activity affects water in different geographic locations.

Focusing attention on patterns helps students to understand the ebb and flow of the systems of which they are a part, and prepares them to engage in studies of other systems—economic, social, political, ecological, and others. Mr. Brown asked his 8th-grade physical education students to chart a professional basketball team's wins by days of the week to see if a pattern existed. It turned out that the team, which had played over 40 games at that point, won all of its games played on Thursdays. His students enjoyed the search for patterns and talked a lot about causation, correlation, and probability, trying to sort them out with Mr. Brown's questioning.

6. VALUING EVIDENCE

Valuing the role of evidence matters. Focusing student attention on evidence produced by classroom investigations sets the stage for learning. Think back to Mr. Rubin's class in Chapter 5, in which students were investigating stones and shells. Providing time in class for finding, using, and analyzing evidence helps students to create relationships between new and previous learnings and to connect dots accurately.

There are many ways in which students are encouraged to find and use evidence: individual assignments, independent study, cooperative teams, small-group work, pair and share protocols, and gallery walks are some examples. These can occur in an array of settings, including online learning platforms, hybrid classes, flipped classrooms, and virtual classes. Teachers use these structures and technologies to support the search for meaning and encourage students to find or generate and use verifiable evidence in their work production.

Think about lessons on the Reconstruction Era after the Civil War, lessons that often prompt students to wonder about the conflicts over civil rights in the United States today. Teachers discuss the issues embedded in Reconstruction and Jim Crow laws, while also asking their students to generate evidence about their impact over time and whether and how their footprints remain visible in today's world. And, of course, the meaning of the law's name. Themes that connect the past to the present, in this case linking the Reconstruction Era of 150 years ago to civil rights today, aren't deviations from the curriculum and aren't tangential—they are directly relevant to the lesson and its broader focus, and they relate to matters students see and hear and read about on news broadcasts and social media sites.

A high school humanities class debated whether installing breathalyzers in newly manufactured automobiles would decrease traffic accidents and deaths, and if so, is it worth the cost of forcing breathalyzers on people who don't consume alcohol? In preparing their positions, students poured over evidence on the federal seat belt law, the polio vaccine, and other legal mandates. These discussions and assignments are important ways of teaching students how to search for and use relevant evidence.

Opportunities to interact with raw data and primary source materials allow students to make conclusions based on evidence, a skill highly valued in most professions, civic life, and living within a household. For example, Mr. Sanchez's high school business class is examining the relationship between health insurance and longevity. Students review raw data on life span in various countries, and insurance coverage rates, and then draw some preliminary conclusions for themselves. This step precedes reading published articles written by respected economists, actuaries, health professionals, and policymakers. Encouraging students to personally construct meaning from primary sources before engaging with texts from experts allows students to feel the exhilaration of seeing patterns emerge from the data, engaging in analyses of the patterns, and constructing an argument or thesis. Moreover, after drawing their own conclusions based on primary source data, students' readings of expert texts are much more critical. Rather than simply accepting the experts' analyses as the most plausible explanations, students often argue with the analyses when they are in conflict with the students' own hypotheses, causing them to engage in further research.

These classes provide very different cognitive experiences than classes based on memorizing information. In contrasting rote memorization, or "mimetic" education, with what he calls a more "transformative" approach to teaching and learning, Gardner (1991) writes:

> In this approach, rather than modeling the desired behavior, the teacher serves as a coach or facilitator, trying to evoke certain qualities or understandings in the students. By posing certain problems, creating certain challenges, placing the student in certain situations, the teacher hopes to encourage the student to work out his own ideas, test them in various ways, and further his own understanding. (p. 119)

7. CONNECTING STUDENTS WITH EACH OTHER

Connecting students with each other matters. Students learn a great deal by speaking with each other. They learn to listen to others' arguments, structure their own arguments, and modify their thinking based on what they hear. It teaches collaboration. It fosters empowerment.

Here is how one middle school art teacher sets the stage for student-to-student interaction that contributes to students' interest in the content of the lesson. Ms. More's class is studying the impact of light. The students are drawing a still life of an arrangement on the table—a vase and flowers. Before beginning their drawings, Ms. More asks students to study the vase and flowers carefully and speak with each other about the aspects of the vase and flowers they will highlight in creating their drawings. In their discussions, some students discuss the shape of the vase, and some focus on the shapes and colors of the flowers. Some mention the shadows cast by the lights in the room and the sunlight peering in through the blinds. Still others wonder whether the flowers would look the same tomorrow if they are unable to finish the drawing today, or if a cloudy day tomorrow would change how the configuration looked. The opportunity for dialogue opened many new ways to think about the vase and flowers and new ways of drawing them.

Students in Mr. Beckett's class are studying the separation of powers in the U.S. government. They have read the Constitution and are now placing certain responsibilities—such as proposing treaties with foreign governments, ratifying those treaties, nominating candidates for the Supreme Court, approving those candidates, vetoing proposed laws, overriding vetoes, and so on—under one of the headings of the three branches of government: executive, legislative, and judicial. Students are working in groups and trying to reach a consensus on where each power resides, talking to each other and consulting the Constitution when needed.

Students in Ms. Ramsey's middle school science class are questioning whether any type of liquid, not only water, can help plants grow. In pairs, students design experiments to test their hypotheses. All pairs agree that their "control" in these experiments will be water and they will add only water to one of their plants. The students determine themselves the liquids to add to their other plants. Some use soda, others use fruit juice, some use the 5% bleach solution used for washing vegetables, and others make a vitamin solution. The students engage in their experiments, and over the course of the next 3 weeks they move around the room to see what their classmates are adding to their plants and the impact it is having on growth. They ask each other questions and explain their thinking to each other. During these 3 weeks, Ms. Ramsey uses the plants of various groups to anchor lessons on photosynthesis and respiration, the equations that describe the processes on the molecular level—the big ideas of the syllabus. When students speak with their classmates about the issues or topics they are studying, knowledge is distributed, communication is increased, and more questions arise. Connecting students also helps students see and connect curricular dots.

Ms. Ramsey knows that big ideas are best taught in authentic situations. She doesn't talk about "plants." She talks about "Harry's and Richard's nasturtium" or "Cara's and Chika's snap peas." Thoughtfully structured investigations and lessons that situate learning in authentic contexts help learners become simultaneously curious and uncertain, and open to new learning. The learning is not necessarily predictable, and different "aha's" of some sort always unfold. But there usually is palpable energy and excitement for both students and teachers; student agency is high, and teachers are promoting enduring learning.

8. POSING TARGETED QUESTIONS

Posing targeted questions matters. There is a difference between "Why do trees in the Northeast bloom in the spring?" and "Would a particularly warm winter cause trees in the Northeast to bloom earlier than normal?" Both questions prompt inquiry, but one adds a layer of specific focus and prediction based on relevant information. Both questions can be engaging, but in many ways, the second question subsumes the first: If teachers or students ask the second question, they also ask the first.

Small changes in question formation can drive different types of thinking. In an elementary school, asking students to state the main idea of a story is a different cognitive activity than asking students to predict what might have happened to certain characters if an element of the story had proceeded differently than the author's version. In a middle school social studies class, asking students to speculate about the various options King George III had in response to the Boston Tea Party is a different cognitive activity than having them read a textbook chapter and restate the king's response. Inviting high school science students to classify organisms by student-determined attributes (e.g., habitat, number of appendages, size, ability to fly, evolutionary relationships, "cute looking") is a different cognitive activity than asking them to memorize the scientific categories of already presorted groups. Reading and stating and restating and memorizing are certainly important skills, and when they develop along with predicting, speculating, and classifying, students grow a rich repertoire of cognitive skills that transfer across disciplines.

Mr. Fitzpatrick discussed the book *Of Mice and Men* (Steinbeck, 1937) with his students. He asked them if George bore any responsibility for placing Lennie in the predicament in which he found himself at the book's conclusion. Students were surprised by the question and went back into the text. Mr. Fitzpatrick also asked if there were earlier opportunities in the story for George to have extricated himself and Lennie from the ranch, an act that may have saved Lennie's life. Students went back again to the text. Some students identified such opportunities, while others did not, and several provocative debates ensued. The nature of the teacher's question prompted the inquiry and discussions. Targeted questions prompt further inquiry. Complex, targeted inquiry gives students opportunities to respond in complex, targeted ways—to look beyond generalities.

9. APPRECIATING CONTEXT

Appreciating context matters. Relevance and interest are linked to context, promote learning, and emerge when the learner's present point of view connects with the lesson.

In a 9th-grade health class, Ms. Lortana conducts a lesson on the relationship between external temperature and muscle movement. Some students raise questions about a slightly different matter—the relationship between physical exercise and muscle movement. They just returned from a physical education class, and that was the context in which their thinking was situated. Ms. Lortana doesn't abandon the original topic. She understands that she can use exercise as a door into body heat, the topic of this lesson, and can also address concepts important in other upcoming units on disease, sleep, and mental health. After inviting her curious students to share their thinking about the relationship between physical exercise and muscle movement, and to develop and conduct an experiment to test their hypotheses, she directs the students' questions about physical exercise back to temperature, a measure of heat. In honoring the context of the students' questions, she allows the lesson to unfold as relevant to students' interests while also working toward the lesson's primary goal.

In Mr. Kurmi's 8th-grade physical science class, some students initially perceived the electricity unit as "scary." But, soon into the lesson, "scary" became "engaging." Students discovered they could use small interlocking electronic blocks to prototype endless innovations that require a complete circuit to run. One student invented and created an electronic nail polish remover using cotton balls on a spinning disk. Another student created a device that used two popsicle sticks to wind a small ball of yarn from a larger ball (for the student's mother who likes to knit). A group of three students worked together to design a model "dance club" with flashing lights and "dancers" made from pipe cleaners on an electronic block that oscillates. Many more inventions were made by students in this class.

Students turned into innovative scientists pursuing their artistic interests (the dance club producers), engineering inclinations (the nail polish remover manufacturer), and compassionate spirits (the mom's yarn spinner fabricator)—while learning the fundamentals of circuitry, power sources, inputs, outputs, connectors, controllers, and current flow. Mr. Kurmi allowed his students to create their own meaningful contexts using electronic building blocks, some popsicle sticks, balls of yarn, cotton balls, and pipe cleaners. In so doing, he made learning accessible, differentiated, rigorous, and transferable.

Consider a high school math class working on solving quadratic equations from a textbook, a problem such as $x^2 + 4x - 21 = 0$. What is x? Most readers of this book, perhaps needing a few online videos to refresh high school memories, could select one of the four common methods of generating the two solutions to the quadratic equation and come up with the solution of (3, −7). Now what? Even with those prompting videos and an answer, most people have constructed little new knowledge about—well, about almost anything related to the original equation. Some readers may be familiar with a newer method recently published by Dr. Po-Shen Loh (Delbert, 2019). Even having correctly generated (3, −7) from his method, many ask: What do these numbers mean? For most, not too much. The problem was presented without a context, and solving it became an exercise in applying a conventional process.

Now consider Ms. Brady's class. They are thinking about and computing with quadratic equations by working on a problem situated in students' everyday lives. The task involves providing data to another class in the school. Mr. Beckett's science class wants to rent a boat on a nearby river to collect native grasses for their experiments. The grasses are 10 km upstream of the school. The river has a current of 2 km per hour. Mr. Beckett thinks it will take about 20 minutes to collect the samples. Mr. Beckett only has a budget to rent the boat for 2 hours. Is a successful trip possible? Can Ms. Brady's math class determine how fast the boat would need to travel and how long each leg of the journey would take, and then advise the science class of the feasibility of the trip? In this case, students are generating quadratic equations appropriate to solve a problem that matters to their schoolmates, and Ms. Brady is guiding the process in accord with her expert knowledge on mathematical procedures.

Two very different approaches to learning how to compute with quadratic equations emerge: One has a local context that sets the stage for strengthening conceptual understanding, and the other does not.

10. CULTIVATING A SENSE OF PLACE

Cultivating a sense of place matters. Structuring lessons around familiar situations, issues, and data provides meaningful contexts that help to generate relevance. Think of the social studies teacher who shows clips of a heated debate among nationally recognized economists to frame a discussion on national policy, or the math teacher who asks her students to assist in computing the cost of building a deck in her backyard, or the middle school music teacher who invites a member of the local community orchestra to play a piece of music with her students and discuss the role music plays in her adult life or the biology teacher who visits the local marsh with her class to study grasses and reeds and their role in the local and global ecosystem. These are experiences related to community—global, national, state, or local—and they respond to context and generate relevance. They are usually perceived as authentic by students because they help them think about ideas important to the worlds in which they live. They develop a sense of place and enable students to be responsive to and responsible for the culture of that place.

Students build ideas with anything and everything: with primary sources such as newspapers, court records, literature, data charts, or personal interviews, or with a variety of three-dimensional materials such as mechanical gears, or living plants, or household chemicals, or with teacher-selected readings, classical experiments, or documentary and fictional films. Materials that enable students to experience objects or data firsthand and manipulate and use them to build transferable ideas are meaningful to students. Opportunities to venture into the local environment, commerce, government, transportation, agriculture, health services, entertainment, and the various industries and activities that comprise their space enable students to build transferable ideas. Although the ability to experience a sense of place contributes significantly to understandings of our immediate and larger worlds, it is the ability to think about and reflect on what we are experiencing that builds knowledge. Teachers who appreciate the vital role of reflecting on one's experiences help students build rich understandings. Richer understandings of the place in which one lives enhances one's sense of belonging and the responsibilities associated with belonging.

Place-based education has a long history of connecting schools with the community and the environment (Sobel, 2013), fostering happy, balanced, healthy lifestyles for children and families (Louv, 2008, 2012), and supporting public engagement in and advocacy of stewardship behavior (Bigelow, 2020).

11. SUPPORTING STUDENT AGENCY

Student agency matters. Students come to school wanting to be recognized as an individual. They crave voice and choice. Most students arrive at school as inquisitive, curious, self-regulating beings who have many ideas and questions about the worlds in which they exist. Sometimes they may appear passive and disinterested, but the active learner still exists inside. No two students think exactly alike, interpret their experiences exactly alike, or understand problems and frame solutions identically. These differences contribute to the richness of schooling.

Some high schools have adopted Socratic Seminars as a way to foster increased student agency—students run the discussions themselves, pose questions to their classmates, and reach conclusions based on their thinking and the contributions of their peers. In a classroom discussion in which high school students are examining what the term "global competence" means, some students see global competence as fostered by classroom lessons related to globally important issues (e.g., climate change, religious differences, famine and poverty, war), while others contend that global competence can only be achieved by venturing out into the world to experience the issues firsthand, in situ. There is no right or wrong answer in this discussion, but a series of comments and questions helps students harden or soften their views and think about their thinking.

Agency also encompasses how students wish to demonstrate what they have learned from their work. This is discussed in greater detail in Chapter 8, but here it is important to recognize that allowing students the freedom to determine the format for showing what they have learned—for example, through a presentation, or a performance, or an exhibition, or a piece of writing, or a drawing—also values students as decisionmakers and invests them more enthusiastically in the process and the product.

Providing opportunities for students to learn content while simultaneously deepening their understanding of themselves as learners are not mutually exclusive. When seen as complementary, they enhance student commitment and reinforce ownership. The gradual release of responsibility from teachers to students (Duke & Pearson, 2002, p. 221) increases greater student investment in their work and ownership of learning while simultaneously enhancing their sense of self-efficacy.

12. NAVIGATING ERROR

Navigating error matters. What adults often call mistakes and misconceptions are the normal intellectual steps of childhood and adolescent concept formation. This was introduced in Chapter 6 with the concept of failing forward, the capacity to learn from error.

Safe spaces enable students to take risks, err, and reboot. Think of scientists in laboratories experimenting with new drugs targeted at specific illnesses: How many times do they unsuccessfully try different approaches that fail? Each failure tells them what doesn't work and brings them to another avenue of inquiry. Think also of young athletes learning to catch a ball with a lacrosse stick. How many times do they miss or drop the ball?

Each attempt brings them one step closer to understanding the right speed, angle, and approach, and to finding success. And, think of the young trombonist trying to get the slide in just the right position to hit a certain note—how many times does she miss the exact spot? Each attempt brings her one step closer to having a feel for the desired arm length, hand placement, and breathing, and to finding success.

Acknowledging with more than a tinge of sarcasm that his suggestion would never be implemented, Postman (1995) put forth this intriguing idea for a "final exam."

> Describe five of the most significant errors scholars have made in (biology, physics, history, etc.). Indicate why they are errors, who made them, and what persons are mainly responsible for correcting them. You may receive extra credit if you can describe an error that was made by the error corrector. You will receive extra extra credit if you can suggest a possible error in our current thinking about (biology, physics, history, etc.). And you will receive extra extra extra credit if you can indicate a possible error in some strongly held belief that currently resides in your mind. (p. 128)

Imagine such an exam! Think of the research and depth of thought that would go into formulating a response, and think of the teaching and learning opportunities.

Cognitive growth is fostered when students are engaged in activities that enable them to revisit and reformulate their conceptions, without judgment. Each new experience either confirms one's perspective, or throws it into doubt, thereby forcing the student to rethink it. Students find confidence in success and/or self-correction.

PART II: GUIDING PRINCIPLES	
Chapter 4 Tying the Learning Frameworks Together	Students make connections across content, deepen reasoning, and construct transdisciplinary knowledge and skills when teachers use the national frameworks to guide lesson development.
Chapter 5 Framing Curricula and Teaching Around Big Ideas	Students think about consequential topics and problems when teachers structure lessons around big ideas, arrange access to appropriate resources, and seek and value students' points of view.
Chapter 6 Fostering the Development of Reasoning With Design Thinking	Students stretch their understanding, creativity, empathy, and resilience with error when teachers engage them in and scaffold authentic design challenges.
Chapter 7 Deepening Reasoning with Transdisciplinary Strategies	Students learn to reason when teachers support student agency; offer worthy problems to solve; connect students to one another; listen; pose targeted questions; offer time to think; seek elaboration on responses; facilitate pattern recognition; and appreciate context, error, place, and evidence.
Chapter 8 Responsibly Assessing Student Learning	

Responsibly Assessing Student Learning

For districts and the schools within them, responsible and meaningful assessment is key in determining next steps for students and a next level of work for schools. This chapter describes responsible assessment, assessments that enable teachers to understand what students know and can do while simultaneously helping students generate new knowledge.

Assessment is not about measuring how much information students are storing in their heads. It's about coming to understand what students know and the extent to which students are able to use and apply the knowledge they are constructing. "Assessment should produce more learning than it measures" (Martin-Kniep, 2014).

Giving information to students and then testing them to determine how much of it they remember, our nation's normative approach to assessment, is a largely wasteful exercise that reveals little about the knowledge the learner has constructed and even less about whether newly constructed knowledge can be transferred and applied to novel situations. The ability to recall facts is a very different cognitive skill than the ability to apply those facts in service to a larger search for meaning. The noted cognitive psychologist, Jerome Bruner, years ago wrote the following. It still rings true today:

> A method of instruction should have the objective of leading the child to discover for himself. Telling children and then testing them on what they have been told inevitably has the effect of producing bench-bound learners whose motivation for learning is likely to be extrinsic to the task—pleasing the teacher, getting into college, artificially maintaining self-esteem. The virtues of encouraging discovery are of two kinds. In the first place, the child will make what he learns his own, will fit his discovery into the interior world of cultures that he creates for himself. Equally important, discovery and the sense of confidence it provides is the proper reward for learning. (1971, pp. 123–124)

Structuring learning as its own reward gives students ownership of the knowledge they construct and assists them in developing the sense of agency and risk-taking needed for unfamiliar situations, even when they recognize that the likelihood of error is high. These are the critical thinkers, creators, innovators, and problem solvers our schools seek to generate.

THE PERILS OF GRADING

Assessing learning within instruction for the purpose of determining next steps is an important way that teachers move learning forward. Grading learning, on the other hand, is a pedagogical dilemma. When teachers assess students to develop a deeper understanding of the students' knowledge, students are free to take risks. When teachers assess students to determine a grade, students often try to mask what they don't know, and teachers are often forced to make difficult decisions.

Wagner and Dintersmith (2015) write:

> if we are committed to meaningful student progress, we need to accept that an entirely different assessment model is required—one that is more qualitative than quantitative, and one that gives up on rank-ordering millions of kids to the nearest tenth of a percentile. . . . We can focus classrooms on what's easiest to measure or on what's most important to learn. But we can't do both well. (p. 226)

Many school districts seek standardization of grading practices. They do so because grading is usually arbitrary and often seems unfair to students and parents. Imagine six 11th-grade classrooms in the same comprehensive high school. In Classroom A, the teacher determines quarterly grades by giving 10 tests/quizzes and averaging the scores. In Classroom B, the teacher determines quarterly grades also by giving 10 tests/quizzes and averaging the scores, but then gives extra credit to students who participate actively in class discussions. In Classroom C, the teacher again computes grades by giving 10 tests/quizzes and averaging the scores, and then deducts points for tardiness to class, lateness in handing in assignments, and/or misbehavior. In Classroom D, the teacher gives just one exam each quarter. In Classroom E, the teacher assigns grades roughly along the bell-shaped curve: 23% get high grades, 23% get low grades, and 54% get grades somewhere in the middle. And, in Classroom F, the teacher believes in giving lower grades early in the year and higher grades as the year progresses in order to demonstrate student growth in learning over the course of the year.

Clearly, there is little "fairness" about these idiosyncratic grading practices. The same student might well get one grade in Classroom A and a different grade in Classroom D. This type of variance is what makes the push for standardized testing so appealing to its proponents—there is one test on which all students are assessed at the same time and in the same way, teachers' idiosyncratic grading practices and judgments are removed, and the playing field is leveled. Except it's not. Trying to level the playing field so that all students can be judged on the same criteria privileges the students who are skilled at the "game" of school, and disadvantages those who are less skilled at it, or choose not to play it.

For teachers, computing a score for a student based on the number of right answers on a test is a simple mathematical process and is far less demanding than providing feedback that helps students contemplate what their next levels of work might be: On a 25-item test, each item is worth 4 points, and the teacher simply counts the number of right answers and multiplies that number by 4. It's easy and simple, and it's also an incomplete and inaccurate way of gauging student knowledge. At its core, it is a deficit model of assessment. Deficit models of assessment inevitably lead to deficit systems of organizing students (i.e., grouping and tracking) and deficit approaches to teaching (e.g., test preparation activities and skills-based remedial instruction).

This teach–test–remediate approach requires teachers to make critical distinctions around specious sets of data and then separate students into groups based on these inappropriate and inaccurate distinctions. It undermines teachers' roles in making context-based decisions in response to more comprehensive evidence about students' learning. It demeans and devalues teachers because it so frequently prevents them from exercising the professional judgment that moves student learning forward.

DATA VERSUS EVIDENCE

When teachers and administrators identify what they value in student learning, they usually point to critical thinking, creativity, collaboration, problem identification and complex problem solving, communication, agility and adaptation, curiosity and imagination (Wagner, 2008), engagement in class lessons and in the broader world, and a palette of dispositions, such as empathy, curiosity, perseverance, questioning, risk-taking and flexible thinking (Kallick & Zmuda, 2017). These are all worthy outcomes, the demonstration of any one of which would make the staff in any school and the parents in any community proud.

Yet, these skills, abilities, and dispositions are rarely the primary intention of most curricular planning and even more rarely documented. Almost all school districts default to documenting success through students' academic attainment on tests. Institutional or community discussion about the outcomes that are valued and how to get better at educating students toward these outcomes is uncommon. Yet, these are essential discussions for school district leaders, faculties, and the general community to have. Greater understanding typically leads to greater support.

There is a difference between data on learning, which today often refer to a set of numbers generated from standardized tests, and evidence of learning, which can take many forms. Evidence on student learning is available every day in schools, gathered by student work samples, observations, conversations, focus groups, or surveys. Evidence collected from multiple sources weaves a more nuanced and more complete story of the programs the school is offering and the learning that is taking place.

Teachers have daily access to evidence by observing students' behaviors, listening to their comments in discussions, and reviewing their work, such as written essays, experimental designs, lab interpretations, and products of multiple media. The challenge for educators is determining the outcomes that are valued, identifying evidence linked to those outcomes, and capturing that evidence in ways that the entire school community can understand.

Some districts use formal protocols to engage faculty in becoming more skillful in capturing evidence related to learning. For example, the *Learning About Student Work (LASW) Protocol* from the National School Reform Faculty (Thompson-Grove, 2000) provides a structure within which teachers and administrators collaboratively identify evidence of reasoning, knowledge, skills, and/or dispositions, with special attention paid to describing, not judging or speculating. Through this and similar protocols, educators collaboratively look at samples of student work, share interpretations of students' sensemaking, and determine implications for classroom practice. This is a productive way to understand what students know and can do, while simultaneously focusing and aligning teacher thinking on the outcomes that matter most. Predating more current research, Newman and colleagues (1989) offered support for this approach:

> Instead of giving the children a task and measuring how well they do or how badly they fail, one can give the children the task and observe how much and what kind of help they need in order to complete the task successfully. In this approach the child is not assessed alone. Rather, the social system of the teacher and the child is dynamically assessed to determine how far along it has progressed. (pp. 77–78)

Several of the learning frameworks described in Chapter 4 highlight systems thinking as a way of understanding part–whole relationships. This certainly is true for schools: Administrators, teachers, students, and parents are essential components of the "system" and can work together to support its development. When adult competencies grow in ways that benefit the system, students grow, creating a fluidity among teaching, learning, and assessment, three significant components of a social system in which educators, students, and parents are complementary players.

CONNECTING TEACHING TO ASSESSING

When students perceive that their thinking is valued, they are much more likely to offer their thoughts publicly. Teachers who offer comments such as "Interesting, tell us more" or "How does that answer connect to what Jane just said?" or "What do the rest of you think about that answer?" not only generate more student thinking and learning, they also uncover evidence of thinking and learning. In classrooms in which students wrestle with questions and challenges, teaching and assessment occur concurrently throughout the lesson.

Conversely, when students perceive there is only one right answer being sought, many withhold their thinking unless they are certain it is correct. To students offering responses, many teachers intend to encourage students with: "Exactly," or "Yes, that's it," or "Perfect." This feedback often inhibits deeper thinking. Teachers who pose comments or proffer questions such as, "Anyone wish to challenge that answer?" or "Is there a different case to be made?" or "How can we be sure?" simultaneously assess what students know while also generating further growth. It is important to encourage students to continue exploring ideas, not to stop when the "right" answer has been acknowledged.

Teaching and assessing are interrelated processes. Teachers interacting with students about their work is a form of informal assessment that generates further learning. Questions such as "How did you get that answer?" or "How did you know to do that?" or "What made you decide to do this instead of that?" or "Is there another way to come at this?" open up windows into students' metacognition, which enables teachers to understand the thinking students employ in addressing classroom work.

These types of questions connect teaching to assessing. Typically, students are asked to reflect on *what* they have learned more than *how* they have learned. Inviting students to examine *how* they learn provides information that helps teachers reach each student, enhancing student agency in the learning process. Some districts capture the "how" by using exit slips, asking students to jot down responses to questions just before leaving class, questions that may be related to a common misconception about the content of that day's lesson, or the process they use at home to study, or questions about the lesson. "What did you learn today?" is a very different question than "How did you learn today?" Both are instructive for teachers, and student responses become evidence on which future lessons are based.

Consider the student who, after being asked how she developed a paper on a particular topic, says, "Well, in trying to understand more about this subject I did some research, and then I made an outline, then I drafted a paper, and then I made edits and did some more research based on the feedback I got, and then did my final draft." In making this statement the student laid out a map of how she learns—relevance, research, organization, feedback, and production. She has narrated her own process, useful for future applications, and the teacher has learned something about how to coach her in future activities.

As students seek to make meaning of seemingly disparate and disconnected ideas and phenomena, they often struggle to understand the extent to which their own cognitive processes are assets and liabilities. Asking students to reflect on how they learn enables them to develop fuller understandings of the ways in which their existing preconceptions, biases, and beliefs affect their openness to new ideas, and how they resolve conflicts between old conceptions and new information.

In Ms. Steele's social studies class, 10th-grader Sarah contended that democracy, as a form of government, isn't working well in the United States. This comment prompted many classmates to disagree. They cited examples of elected representation, freedom of speech, and other structures that they thought are working the way the Constitution intended. A discussion of governmental processes ensued, involving questions posed by the teacher and other students in the class, and Sarah came back into the conversation with, "I actually know the difference between the ideal and real—why didn't I listen to myself?" It was an important question in her growth as a thinker and learner. She reformulated her argument as she and the class dug deeper into the tenets and practices of the U.S. government.

ASSESSMENT THAT GENERATES STUDENT THINKING

There are some intriguing methods of generating student thinking through assessment. One is beginning with the "right" answer and asking students to determine how that answer is reached. Another is preparing for a question. Let's see them in action.

Begin With the Answer

In Ms. O'Connor's 2nd-grade math class, students are writing number expressions for the number 139—it is the 139th day of the school year. The challenge is to write number expressions that include the four basic operations of elementary math: addition, subtraction, multiplication, and division. The students in this class have been doing this activity for several weeks with other numbers—for example, 127 on the 127th day of the year. On day 139, they write a wide variety, with surprisingly little overlap. See Figure 8.1.

Sometimes Ms. O'Connor organizes lessons around producing one accurate computation with multiple parts, and at other times she structures lessons that promote the search for multiple pathways to one right answer. The expressions in Figure 8.1 are examples of multiple paths to the right answer which, in this case, was already known by the students: 139. Asking students to write number expressions leading to the already-known answer demands different cognitive processes than giving students numbers and asking them to compute the sum—which is the normative mathematical

Figure 8.1. Students' Math Expressions

$[(60 \times 2) + 15 + (4 \times 1)]$
$[(30 \times 3) + (80 \div 2) + (13 - 4)]$
$(75 + 100 - 36)$
$[(5 \times 5 \times 5) + 14]$
$[(45 \div 5) + 81 + 9 + (200 \div 5)]$

procedure in most classes and on most tests. Starting with the sum permits students to focus their attention on the operations that lead to that sum: in other words, to think conceptually like a mathematician while simultaneously engaging in computation practice.

Accurate computation is undeniably important in math, and it is imperative for teachers to understand how to foster its development. The students in Ms. O'Connor's class are computing with increasingly sophisticated proficiency and efficiency while also solidifying their understanding of mathematical concepts. They are honing their capacities to combine and recombine numbers, hold equivalencies in mind, and computationally manipulate numbers using adding, subtracting, multiplying, and dividing, all by considering ways to generate the number 139.

By asking students to construct expressions and equations themselves rather than doing it for them, Ms. O'Connor assesses their individual skills and understandings, while simultaneously generating a good deal of student interest, excitement, and continued learning. Also of note is that the 2nd-graders in this class are seeing relationships among the four basic operations of math. In most schools, 2nd-graders have not yet been formally taught multiplication and division. In this class, they are constructing for themselves beginning versions of the algorithms.

The "known answer" approach is effective in all content areas. For example, the relationship between the Earth and its moon is always a source of both interest and confusion for students and adults. Most students are surprised to learn that we always see the same side of the moon, no matter where we stand on Earth and no matter what time of day or night. The teacher asks for an explanation. In this lesson, the teacher begins with the observed phenomenon, or, the "right" answer—we always see the same side of the moon—and invites students to use any resource to explain the phenomenon. Students excitedly engage in the search, and put forward many seemingly reasonable, but often inaccurate explanations. Getting to the accurate explanation that the rotation of the moon on its own axis and its revolution around the Earth is a 1:1 ratio, and getting all members of the class to understand it well enough to explain it to others, is typically a long process no matter how many props are rotated and revolved, google searches conducted, or textbook passages read. Almost always, in the end, students' interest and engagement, scaffolded by the teacher, lead them to the explanation, with widened eyes and applause when everyone agrees.

Another example—In discussing Shakespeare's *Othello*, the teacher challenges her students: "We know Iago is considered a villainous character. Can you support that case based on evidence in the story, or can you make a different case?" The answer is already known—Iago is a villain—and the students' quest is to find supporting or refuting evidence. Counter to the normative methods of teaching the causes leading to a widely accepted interpretation, this method is a powerful tool for the construction of knowledge because the "answer" is already known, and the task of the students is not to discover the "right" answer but instead to defend or refute this interpretation.

Prepare for the Question

Different from beginning with an answer, but equally engaging, is preparing for a question. Mr. Wilson, a veteran high school chemistry teacher, has spent much of his career giving January midterm exams consisting of factual multiple-choice, short-answer, and fill-in questions. After several discussions with his school principal, who is trying to move the faculty to more constructivist approaches with students, Mr. Wilson decides to jettison his midterm exam in favor of a new process that he and the principal think will better assess what students actually know about chemistry.

Mr. Wilson is eager to find out. During the first semester's work leading up to the new midterm assessment, he identified 13 big ideas embedded in the chemistry curriculum and told students that over the last 2 weeks of January he would meet with each of them individually for 5 minutes (he teaches about 75 students in three sections) to discuss in some detail two of the 13 big ideas. The students would not know in advance which two big ideas they would discuss with Mr. Wilson—on the day of the meeting they each would randomly select 2 topics (on index cards) from among 13, and those would be the focus of their discussions. When January arrived, the school provided a substitute teacher for 2 days, and Mr. Wilson met with each of his students individually during that time.

After the meetings, students reported to Mr. Wilson that they had spent much more time seeking to understand the big ideas in preparation for the midterm interview than they had spent memorizing information for previous science tests. They also shared that they learned even more about the two topics they selected through the questions he posed during their 5-minute conversations with him. Several reported that they were disappointed they only had 5 minutes and could only discuss two topics. Mr. Wilson reported that he learned more about students' knowledge of chemistry concepts by talking with them (for only 5 minutes each) than he had ever learned through administering and scoring midterm exams. It was a revelation that changed how he teaches.

PERFORMANCE ASSESSMENT

Another prominent way to surface what students know and can do is through performance assessment. Tests ask the question: "Do you know *this?*" "This" is defined by the maker of the test—the state education department, a publisher, or a classroom teacher: Whoever creates the test defines what is important to know.

Performance assessments ask the question: "*What* do you know?" It's a very different question. In response to "Do you know *this?*" the answer is either yes or no: Students either pass with gradations or fail the test. In response to "*What* do you know?" all students know something, and the performance assessment enables them to demonstrate what they know and guides their teachers in determining next teaching steps.

When "Do you know *this?*" is the only question being asked of students, the test yields only a partial picture of what students know and can do, and privileges those who resonate with the testing format while disadvantaging those who do not. Adding "*What* do you know?" to the mix paints a more comprehensive picture of each student's knowledge.

It is important to note that the "*this*" in testing is controlled by the adult who makes the test, while the "*what*" in performance assessment is usually controlled by the student—students make decisions about what information, style, and format will be meaningful in creating the performance and demonstrate aspects of their knowledge and skills through those decisions.

There are endless examples of performance assessments. In an economics elective course, a student may generate a recommendation for the purchase of a new car that is safe, gets good mileage per gallon of gasoline, is economically feasible, and is comfortable. In an English class, a student may develop a plan for making the school "greener" and create a presentation to the local board of education. In a 3rd-grade class, students may create welcoming habitats for threatened species.

Performance-based assessments are usually student-driven, long-range, interdisciplinary, research-based activities in which students have a choice in both topic and presentation format: performances, products, exhibitions, demonstrations, or showcases that enable students to convey what they know. Opportunities for other students and adults to comment and ask questions are often included, deepening the learning of both presenter and audience.

In Mr. Cavallero's class, one group of students is preparing to ship supplies, some of which are breakable, to a partner school on another continent. Students have already researched the cost and time frame of international shipping and are figuring out how to send the supplies in the least number of small boxes. Mr. Cavallero suggests that they evaluate their packing of the fragile valuables by doing some pilot testing with low-cost fragile items. The students decide that they will build cartons to determine the least amount of packing that would keep a potato chip from breaking.

Different groups of students work on producing a matrix of materials, cost, shape, and size of the packages. Mr. Cavallero is assessing leadership skills, computer skills, initiative, executive functioning, content knowledge, creativity, critical thinking, problem solving, perseverance, and many other skills and dispositions. Having students work on authentic, often transdisciplinary tasks makes seeking disconnected measures of achievement, such as tests, seem not only unnecessary, but counterproductive to the flow of learning.

Most teachers who document learning with performance-based assessments use a rubric, a scoring tool that lists criteria for the successful completion of the assignment and its grading. Rubrics often serve as road maps for students so they can self-assess their work, and also explanations of teacher grading in discussions with students and parents. There are mixed views about the use of rubrics. Well used, rubrics are specific to the work in which students are engaged, and skillful teachers offer them with intention. They can generate self-regulation, broad thinking, and opportunities to expand one's work. Less well used, however, rubrics often generate compliance with preestablished processes and constrain student experimentation. Students comply to varying degrees with the steps, activities, and behaviors listed on the rubrics and receive grades based on the extent and quality of their compliance. Students learn about the topic they studied, but the need to conform to preestablished processes and follow specific sequences denies them the agency involved in making essential decisions about what is important and how to portray that importance.

RESPONSIBLE ASSESSMENT

John Merrow has invited educators to change an essential assessment question from "How intelligent is this child?" to "How is this child intelligent?" (2019, para. 16)—the same five words but two very different questions. Responsible assessment makes this important shift and moves learning forward. The Tri-State Consortium, an alliance of dozens of school districts in New York, New Jersey, and Connecticut, has worked for decades to assist educators in assessing student knowledge. The Consortium developed a set of principles relating to responsible assessment (Tri-State Consortium, 2020). These principles provide a framework for assessing student learning and are aligned with a constructivist approach to teaching and assessing. They recognize the dynamic interplay between learning and teaching, urge that assessment be used as a process to gauge student learning and adjust teaching accordingly, and recognize that assessments and the data they generate have limits that, when exceeded, can be harmful. See Figure 8.2.

These principles of responsible assessment have underpinned over 150 school district visits conducted by the Tri-State Consortium, have helped educators in these districts to look broadly at the impact of both curriculum

Figure 8.2. Principles of Responsible Assessment

Tri-State Consortium

Principles Regarding Responsible Assessment and the Appropriate Use of Assessment Data

Principle 1: Purpose of Responsible Assessment

The purpose of assessment is to give students opportunities to demonstrate their understanding of content, concepts, and skills and to provide feedback to students in order to improve their learning. Responsible assessments enable educators to generate and analyze information about student learning, and to alter the teaching–learning dynamic to better meet students' needs. Responsible assessment measures the effect of and informs curriculum and instruction. In general terms, schools ask students to acquire information, apply and transfer knowledge, and construct understandings. Responsible assessment generates information about the extent to which students can do all three.

Principle 2: Forms of Responsible Assessment

Assessment may be diagnostic, formative, or summative. All three forms have limitations and should not be used as the sole indicators of student learning. Multiple forms of assessment provide a broader and more accurate picture of what students know and can do. Standardized tests are useful in examining the learning of large groups of students and assisting educators and the public to make comparisons and identify patterns within and across groups of students, while more authentic, performance-based assessments are helpful in providing richer detail about what individual students know and can do and how they progress over time.

Principle 3: Misuse of Responsible Assessment

Assessments designed to provide information about individual student learning should not be used to gauge the effectiveness of schools or school districts, or the competence of teachers. Just as it is inappropriate to make judgments about students based on any single measure, it is also inappropriate to make judgments about teachers, schools, or school districts based on any single measure.

Principle 4: Characteristics of Responsible Assessment

Responsible assessment is valid, reliable, meaningful and, to the extent possible, authentic. Authentic assessments are transdisciplinary and invite students to engage in higher-order thinking. They generate results that are replicable across populations and information about learning that is meaningful for students and teachers alike. This information may be quantitative and/or qualitative. Responsible assessment strikes a balance between standardized measures and more authentic, performance-based measures. The information gathered through authentic assessment is to be used in conjunction with data gathered through norm-referenced and criterion-referenced tests to develop a fuller and richer picture of student knowledge and understanding.

(*continued*)

Figure 8.2. (*continued*)

Principle 5: Variations Within Responsible Assessment

Different people learn in different ways and at different rates. Responsible assessment honors this reality by acknowledging learning at specific moments in time, by accounting for growth in learning over time, and by generating information that sheds light on students' learning in relation to self and in relation to external standards.

Principle 6: Equity in Responsible Assessment

Responsible assessment accounts for the inevitable variations in students' cultural and socioeconomic backgrounds and experiences, language differences, and abilities and disabilities. One size does not fit all students equally, and responsible assessment recognizes that some students are advantaged and disadvantaged by reliance on only one form of assessment.

Principle 7: Professional Understanding of Responsible Assessment

All forms of assessment have strengths and limitations. Those developing and administering assessments must understand the basic tenets contained in this set of principles. It is the responsibility of the institutions in which they work to provide ongoing professional learning opportunities focused on assessment and the use of assessment data.

Principle 8: Revision and Refinement of Responsible Assessment

Responsible assessment practices must be regularly reviewed and revised in order to remain relevant for the students participating in them and instructionally informative for the educators administering them.

and instruction, and have reminded educators that teacher and student voice and agency are essential factors in learning. Assessment is most meaningful when it is in service to the learner.

CHANGING THE NARRATIVE

Although learning is the essence of classroom life, students' internal learning processes remain invisible. Teachers can only see products of learning. When students grapple with meaningful, complex problems, they are engaging in opportunities through which they may or may not transform previous cognitive understandings into newly adapted ones. Teachers watch and listen and try to understand what students are learning and guide them based on observations. But what is happening mentally with each student remains largely unknown.

Significantly, this ongoing, recursive process of learning is linked to an ongoing, recursive process of assessment. Students, every day, encounter numerous opportunities to engage with people, places, ideas, objects, and situations: How will I come at this assignment; how will I choose the topic to study; how will I establish my role in this group; how will I determine when to take intellectual risks; what resources will I use; and how will I demonstrate what I've learned. As students make these decisions—and many others—and interact with one another, their teachers witness multiple incidences of critical thinking, creative thinking, collaboration, perseverance, problem solving, flexibility, kindness to others, empathy, curiosity, and communication—all of the worthy outcomes valued by their school districts.

The evidence exists, but systematically capturing evidence of students' behaviors and work products for every student every day is a cumbersome task for one teacher working with a full class. In fact, trying to do so actually interferes with instruction—not unlike the notion that a thermometer increases or decreases the temperature of whatever it is measuring. Assessing something changes it. But there are ways to note, document, and monitor instances of behaviors and work products with unobtrusive, mindful, descriptive, nonjudgmental language—and numbers, too, if desired—as illustrated by Ms. Steele, Ms. O'Connor, Mr. Wilson, Mr. Cavallero, and the other teachers presented in this chapter. Doing so changes the narrative from test scores as proxies for learning to more estimable outcomes and enables districts to tell the more meaningful stories they want their communities to hear.

Districts' stories are significant, as are the stories of the teachers, administrators, and students within them. In a TED Talk, Brené Brown shared, "Maybe stories are just data with a soul" (2010, 1:04). We wonder the same, which makes telling the right stories so important—not the stories told by test data that are disconnected from school districts' missions, but the stories that connect directly to those missions, the stories that are embedded in the bountiful and revelatory evidence of student learning that exists in every classroom every day.

This chapter closes Part II of this book. Part III, Stepping Up and Speaking Out, includes two chapters that discuss norms and structures in schools that either foster or impede a constructivist approach to education and actions educators can take to move education in this direction.

PART II: GUIDING PRINCIPLES	
Chapter 4 Tying the Learning Frameworks Together	Students make connections across content, deepen reasoning, and construct transdisciplinary knowledge and skills when teachers use the national frameworks to guide lesson development.
Chapter 5 Framing Curricula and Teaching Around Big Ideas	Students think about consequential topics and problems when teachers structure lessons around big ideas, arrange access to appropriate resources, and seek and value students' points of view.
Chapter 6 Fostering the Development of Reasoning With Design Thinking	Students stretch their understanding, creativity, empathy, and resilience with error when teachers engage them in and scaffold authentic design challenges.
Chapter 7 Deepening Reasoning With Transdisciplinary Strategies	Students learn to reason when teachers support student agency, offer worthy problems to solve, connect students to one another, listen, pose targeted questions, offer time to think, seek elaboration on responses, facilitate pattern recognition, and appreciate context, error, place, and evidence.
Chapter 8 Responsibly Assessing Student Learning	Students develop voice and agency when teachers incorporate responsible assessment into instruction and encourage students to demonstrate what they know and can do through multiple means.

STEPPING UP AND SPEAKING OUT

CHAPTER 9

Shifting Norms and Structures

In order for any change in teaching and learning to take hold in a school, the structures and norms that frame the organization's culture must support the change. When alignment among these elements is tight, a powerful and seamless message about what is valued ripples through the system. When norms and structures are misaligned with the desired change, they impede it, surfacing as roadblocks, eliciting questions about the extent to which schools are committed to the change. This chapter examines common school norms and structures that must be considered when opening space for students' construction of knowledge and meaning.

In considering a shift, all aspects of a school day are open for discussion. For example, master schedules are important. Do students need more time to think and design than traditional bell schedules afford? Curricula are important because the "what" needs to match the "how," working together to encourage student exploration and reflection. Differentiation is important because learning is enhanced when each student's uniqueness is recognized and valued. Space is important because it influences creativity, design, and collaboration. Professional learning is important because it enables teachers to connect repertoires of practice with the desired change. And supervision and evaluation are important because analysis of the work being implemented is essential to the professional growth of teachers and supervisors, and the functioning of the system.

VISIONING AND VALUING

Earlier sections of this book have discussed the importance of thinking big, structuring curriculum around big ideas that matter to students, and understanding that learning is maximized when curricula are presented whole-to-part, not part-to-whole. Just as thinking big is critical in teaching and learning, so, too, is it essential in visioning and valuing, and in the systemic leadership that frames these processes.

Michael Fullan (2001, 2003, 2011) has written extensively about the role of leadership in establishing meaningful district visions. One of the points he and other organizational change theorists make about leadership

Figure 9.1. Focusing on Big Issues

	UNITY OF PURPOSE	DIVISIVENESS
BIG ISSUES	Vision ———— Transformation	Ideological conflict ———— Exploration
SMALL ISSUES	Discrete unlinked decisions ———— Stagnation	Interpersonal conflict ———— Regression

is the need to keep the school community focused on the large ideas that frame a district's vision. Figure 9.1 illustrates the relationship between focusing on big issues and small issues. When organizations focus on smaller ideas, even with unity of purpose, the system stagnates because discrete, unlinked decisions are being made and little of significance is occurring. However, attending to large, consequential matters brings about either ideological conflict (which is positive because it leads to further exploration) or a unified vision (which results in transformation).

District visions frequently change as leaders come and go. Over time, some, perhaps many, faculty members become inured to constantly changing visions and learn to ignore and even resist them. They understandably focus their energies instead on their own classrooms and their own ways of teaching because those are the settings in which they are most comfortable and the behaviors and activities over which they have the most control.

Teacher voice must be at the heart of any change in approach. If you ask teachers how students learn, they'll tell you, and if you ask them if their districts' visions are impactful, they'll tell you that, too. Crafting a vision without their input and support usually renders the vision meaningless— words on a page that have no impact on the daily work of teachers and students. Thus, moving from one teaching approach to another must be done *with* teachers, not *to* them. It is culture-changing work that affects every aspect of the educational environment. Susan Moore Johnson (2005) wrote:

> One can reasonably argue that teachers who have little or no say in determining the policies and practices of their schools cannot effectively educate students to live in a democratic society. For when there are excessive constraints on teachers' authority within the school, students may dismiss lessons about access and equity that are taught in the formal curriculum, absorbing instead lessons about compliance, deference, and impotence that are conveyed by the hidden curriculum. (p. 160)

Acknowledging the indispensable role of teachers in both creating and/ or reshaping a district's vision increases the odds that vision-related work will be enacted by them. Some leaders resist engaging teachers because doing so will almost always slow the process of change and result in mutual adaptation (McLaughlin, 1976), a reciprocal process through which the planned change will alter teaching and the teachers will alter the planned change. Rather than being resisted, however, mutual adaptation is an aspect of organizational change that deserves embracing because it mirrors student learning—new information alters the ways in which students think, and students' thinking alters the way in which the information is understood. It's how humans, and organizations, grow.

ESTABLISHING A CULTURE OF LEARNING

Opportunities for professional learning related to vision are essential. Just as constructivist teachers negotiate curricula with students rather than "delivering" it, professional learning must follow the same approach. If a district wants its teachers to value the thinking of students, the district must value the thinking of its teachers in the same way.

Professional learning is multidirectional, and creating time for it is always a concern. Some districts, either through early dismissal or late arrival days for students, open up more time for their faculties' professional learning, using this time for sharing and analyzing teaching practices. Other districts create professional learning communities (PLCs) within which teachers examine students' work together. Still other districts hire classroom coaches to help teachers focus on specific aspects of their instructional practices. Other approaches to professional learning involve common planning, teaming, department meetings, and whole faculty meetings linked to implementation of desired practices (Jacobs & Alcock, 2018). And, of course, many teachers continue their own education through certificate and degree granting programs at colleges and universities.

There are significant differences between the ideas and behaviors that underpin more traditional settings and those in constructivist settings, ranging from curriculum to instruction to assessment to the role students play in their own learning. Figure 9.2 summarizes some of the more visible differences between these learning environments.

These differences are reflective of two distinct cultures. Moving from a more traditional to a more constructivist school environment rests on the collective will to make this shift: the ongoing professional learning of all educators, both teachers and administrators, as well as the education of parents and the larger community.

Figure 9.2. A Look at School Environments

More Traditional	More Constructivist
Curriculum is presented part-to-whole, with emphasis on improving basic skills.	Curriculum is presented whole-to-part, with emphasis on enhancing understanding of big ideas.
Strict adherence to and coverage of fixed curricula are highly valued.	Pursuit of student interests and contextual questions are valued as a launch point and context for learning.
Curricular activities rely heavily on textbooks and workbooks.	Curricular activities rely heavily on primary sources of data, the natural world, student-selected materials, and personal experiences.
Students are viewed as receivers of information needing external motivators and reinforcement.	Students are viewed as self-motivated, self-regulated thinkers with emerging theories about the world.
Teachers generally behave as sources of content, disseminating information to students.	Teachers generally behave as content facilitators, mediating environments for students' discoveries, often within design challenges.
Teachers rely on tests to document student learning.	Teachers seek students' points of view to document student learning and assist in determining subsequent lessons.
Assessment of student learning is viewed as separate from teaching.	Assessment is interwoven with teaching and occurs through observation of students at work and through student performances, products, exhibitions, and portfolios.
Students primarily work alone or in groups with predefined roles set by the teacher.	Students primarily work collaboratively in groups, determining for themselves how to work most efficiently and effectively.

ALIGNING CURRICULA

Some packaged curricula come with inflexible scripts and pacing guides for teachers to follow, emphasizing structure and content while limiting teachers' decisionmaking in classrooms. Tightly controlled curricula, while promoting horizontal and vertical alignment of content, often militate against the teacher and student autonomy needed for concept building. Because constructivist teaching promotes both sensemaking around content and agency over one's learning, rigidly scripted curricula usually are not amenable to this approach.

As students move from elementary to middle to high school, transitions often carry abrupt shifts in both curriculum and instructional practices that pose subtle or significant challenges for students. For example, many districts use a conceptually oriented elementary math curriculum, a procedural, textbook/workbook-oriented middle school math curriculum, and separate course-based high school math sequences—three distinct approaches within the same school system. One 6th-grader, in discussing the shift from his elementary math program to his middle school program, said: "It's the difference between thinking and memorizing." Indeed.

These are major changes for many students, perpetuating the notion that while the elementary years are a playful time in which student interest and voice are valued, the middle and high school years are when students enter "the real world" in which the search for personal meaning is subordinated to the "rigor" of mastering content. This view interferes with the growth of human potential. Conceptually oriented curricula stimulate learning across an unfolding continuum.

Thus, it is important for districts to examine the extent to which the curricula they use, at all levels, are amenable to a constructivist approach to learning. On a recent peer-review visit to a school district, a member of the visit team asked, "What is the writing life of a student in this district?" This question generated a good deal of discussion. In response, the district's faculty recognized that the writing life of students changed dramatically as they moved through the system, with some parts of that life promoting the construction of knowledge more than others. The question caused the faculty to investigate how curricular inconsistencies affect students.

Another alignment issue for districts to consider is the extent to which the written curriculum, the taught curriculum, and the assessed curriculum are linked (Glatthorn, 2004). In some districts, what is written is different from what is taught, and what is taught is different from what is assessed. It is challenging to teach a constructivist-aligned curriculum in a setting in which student learning is assessed solely through conventional testing. The tests will not assess much of what the students have been doing and may be misaligned with how they have been doing it. Teaching for thinking and assessment for thinking can be complementary and productive endeavors when the system works at matching them.

COLLABORATING WITH PARENTS

Some parents, especially those educated in more traditional schools, may not immediately resonate with constructivist pedagogy. For example, the concept of failing forward is unfamiliar to many parents who don't always perceive it as a step toward success. Also, flattening the hierarchies embedded in traditional tracking and grading takes away the widely accepted structures on which some parents of high-achieving students, as well as the students themselves, have learned to rely—that's the model they know and the model that has benefited them. To some parents, constructivism is counterintuitive to their understanding of how learning occurs and schools are organized.

However, it also is true that most parents want their children to have greater agency, to spend time thinking critically and creatively about worthy ideas, to identify and try to resolve authentic, complex problems, to be fully engaged in meaningful activities, to work effectively both independently and with others, and to be prepared for the complexities of the world into which they will graduate. They value curiosity and perseverance, and a host of other dispositions associated with self-regulation.

Of course, parents also want high test scores, college acceptances, and productive careers and lives for their children. High test scores and constructivist classrooms are not mutually exclusive. But this story needs narration from district and school leaders, and especially from classroom teachers who are tied most closely with parents and on whom parents rely for reassurance.

Cultural transitions require parental engagement from the start so that parents have time to ponder the ideas and contribute to the process. There exist some misconceptions about constructivism, its practices, and its goals. These myths are best dispelled through direct experience, when parents understand what is occurring, why it is occurring, and see their children succeeding and thriving. Transparent policies, welcoming schools, and opportunities for parent voices to be heard encourage collaboration, which most parents value.

In many regions, parents and community members vote on their district's budget. It is useful for districts to examine the extent to which the annual budget supports the constructivist vision the district is communicating to parents, community members, and staff. This is another area that can benefit from narration to help parents understand the depth and complexity of the district's story.

DIFFERENTIATING FOR EQUITY

Constructivism describes the way in which we each make meaning of our worlds. All students and adults construct meaning, whether schools are structured to encourage that or not. It's what humans do naturally, before school, during school, and after school. What makes teaching so complicated is that we don't all construct the same meanings, and we don't all do it in the same ways or at the same times, which strengthens the need for differentiation. Differentiation of instruction requires understanding each student's strengths as a learner and targeting schoolwork to those strengths in order to maximize the likelihood of engagement and learning. This is time consuming and sophisticated work, and vastly different from teaching targeted to an entire class.

All districts grapple with ways to differentiate. Sometimes teachers prepare assignments for students to work on individually. Sometimes teachers group students fluidly, changing groups based on students' evolving thinking about the concepts under study. As was seen in the classrooms of teachers described in previous chapters, groups may work on the same concept in different contexts or on different concepts within the same context. Teachers negotiate the scope and sequence of the curricula based on students' thinking.

Some districts view differentiation as a group enterprise through tracking, separating students into perceived ability groups. This approach to differentiation carries some concerns, including the predictable shrinking of options for some students as their academic careers progress. Tracking can begin as early as the 3rd grade, almost always for math instruction. However, at the age of 7 or 8, developmental readiness plays a significant role in mathematical thinking, and it is difficult to distinguish between developmental readiness and unfolding academic potential. For most students, placement in low, middle, or high groups becomes their destiny: The vast majority of students remain in these tracks throughout their academic careers, irrespective of subsequent academic growth or burgeoning interest.

For many of these students, by the time they are developmentally ready to tackle more complex curricula, their opportunity for participation in their districts' most advanced courses has passed—with significant long-term repercussions (Mathews, 1998; Oakes, 2005). Access to what is considered "rigorous curriculum" is linked to options later in life—postsecondary school, the subjects in which one majors, career choices, earning potential and, ultimately, lifestyle possibilities. The stakes in tracking are high.

Differentiation through tracking versus differentiation through personalization and grouping is a thorny issue in which historical inequities, pedagogical decisions, and life goals coalesce. Students of lower socioeconomic means, often students of color and nonnative English speakers, take honors or Advanced Placement courses in much smaller percentages than their wealthier, native English-speaking peers. Because most tests are culturally biased, and for reasons having nothing to do with intellect or ability, these students statistically score lower on standardized measures than do more affluent students, and these lower scores usually result in prerequisites not being met and fewer teacher recommendations for placement in advanced courses.

This practice results in disproportionality—institutionally discriminatory procedures, frequently unintentional—that deny specific subgroups of students equitable access to advanced curriculum. Lower wealth students and nonnative English speakers are most often disadvantaged, carrying forward historical inequities. Thus, when schools place these students in classes where they are perceived to have the greatest likelihood of success—that is, in lower tracks—the schools actually continue to perpetuate a permanent underclass of students.

Two actions can mitigate this situation somewhat. First, schools can delay tracking students, certainly through the elementary and early middle school years. Doing this keeps doors open for greater numbers of students for longer periods of time. Second, permitting students to self-select into courses in the middle and high school years gives them both voice and choice.

The pedagogy of constructivism cannot solve the equity and access concerns associated with tracking. Tracking involves institutional and political policies laced with cultural issues. But the pedagogy of constructivism can definitely speak to what is commonly called rigor. Rigor is not related to the level of the course: It is embedded in the work students are invited to do. Students can be challenged to construct meaning in every course, irrespective of level or course title. It is the pedagogy of classes in conjunction with the skillfulness of the teacher and the engagement of the students that determine rigor, relevance, and equity.

CONSIDERING SPACE AND TIME AND TECHNOLOGY

Spaces designed to promote students as creators often mirror workshop and laboratory-type settings that allow students to work collaboratively with classmates. To be inclusive, physical spaces that consider lighting, accessibility, ventilation, color, vistas, storage, and technology are usually the ones that welcome the greatest numbers of students and teachers—and visitors. Who doesn't like to see a cool school?

Today, innovative thinking about space also includes virtual spaces that consider access to equipment and curricular materials, family support, and the costs of providing technology and hotspots where none exist in the family. The settings in which learning occurs must be consistent with the type of learning being promoted and the desired outcomes. In addition to flexible seating and movable furniture, fresh air and natural ambient light and spaces for different types of activities are necessary for physical space and movement that can promote safe collaboration. For health reasons on many levels, the need for outdoor spaces in all climates is increasing along with the need for spaces that provide privacy and allow for synchronous connections among families and teachers.

Because the personal construction of knowledge is messier, more complex, and more time intensive than information exchange and note-taking, the way in which learning time is structured and how students move from setting to setting throughout the day are key factors. Whether offering instruction in person or remotely, research on how students learn invites us to reexamine scheduling to accommodate learner-centered investigations that occur over time. Project-oriented work and performance-based assessments encourage teachers to expand and vary their teaching repertoires. Jacobs and Alcock (2018) have written persuasively about these matters and a host of other related shifts in classroom pedagogy with rich classroom examples.

David Thornburg (2013), influenced by Piaget, Vygotsky, and Papert, suggests that schools re-create their spaces to serve four different metaphoric functions: "campfire spaces" for learning from experts or performers; "watering holes" for conversational learning among peers; "caves" for quiet reflective learning with oneself; and "life," places in which students apply and transform what they've learned. To varying degrees, these designs underpin the work of many of today's school architects (Nair et al., 2009). Of course, finances may dictate how "beautiful" or "bedazzling" the spaces may be, and social distancing mandates due to infectious disease controls cause constraints. But it is pedagogy and the people who enact it that dictate how inspirational, useful, and effective these spaces are.

The development of the World Wide Web in the 1990s transformed learning for students and life for people across the globe. Not only is technology everywhere today, but the entirety of the outside world exists virtually in everyone's pocket. We pull out our cell phones to check on the weather, look up words we don't know, find directions to new addresses, count the number of steps we've taken in a day, monitor our heart rates, and write a reminder note. Cell phones, tablets, laptop computers, and smartwatches, all connected to the web, have changed everything from teaching and parenting to business and commerce. The web and the devices we use to access it have changed relationships of all types. And then the COVID-19 pandemic swept in and added yet another layer of meaning to the impact of technology on schooling.

Both in and out of schools, students can and regularly do use their devices to generate compelling experiences: They hold conversations with people in other lands and visit historic sites; tap into data sources to support or refute arguments; and watch live debates and discussions about topics of relevance. Many students code, create games, and simulate events that interest and intrigue them. They also purchase virtually any good and/or service. The possibilities are limitless and, when used effectively, technology expands students' worlds.

Of course, danger lurks as well, and students can wander into murkier waters. Schools have developed various safeguards to minimize these dangers, but another caution exists. Often, interactions with the outside world overtake interactions with people near us in the moment. Most of us certainly have witnessed this occurrence or have been part of it: people constantly connected to their devices but not emotionally connected to others in the room. Meaningful conversation among people, and the empathy and relationships that conversations foster, are in decline due to the omnipresence and compelling attraction of digital connections (Turkle, 2015). Clearly the addictive nature of virtual gaming, the constancy of social media, and multitasking at all hours of the day can overwhelm relationships of all kinds and can interfere with mindful attention in school.

Ironically, at a time that society is grappling with ways to balance device use with human conversation, the global health pandemic of 2020 made devices indispensable tools in establishing and maintaining human conversation during mandated social distancing, a mandate that has required celebrations, conferences, meetings, retreats, yoga classes, weddings, and funerals, all previously events for device-free interactions, to take place *through* devices. And, of course, schooling, too.

The mandated closing of schools during the global health pandemic of 2020 catapulted common usages of technologies into distance learning platforms in ways and to a scale never before anticipated—with unknown projections for its future use. Remarkably, reinventing schools as platforms for distance learning took place in just 2 weeks during March 2020, as the nation and world became aware of its massive battle with novel coronavirus. With unexpected suddenness, remote learning has become a pillar on which education relies during times of necessary social distancing. In making these shifts we have learned lessons that have broadened our definition from school as a place to school as a concept.

SCHOOL AS A CONCEPT

Distance learning cannot replace the power, beauty, energy, and human connection of face-to-face interaction in schools. No one expects or wants that. But, in the absence of or with limits on face-to-face learning, distance learning can share the same goal—enduring learning. That common goal serves as a guide in creating settings in which teachers and parents become members of conversations *with* students rather than speakers *to* students, and students become informed contributors to the learning platform, not consumers of it, whether it be a classroom or a screen view.

Expanding the use of distance learning reminds us to look carefully at the structures and curricula we set up, particularly how closely they are tied to research on how people learn. For young children, play is a condition for learning (Fromberg & Bergen, 2015). Play helps children test and symbolize their growing knowledge and build academic competence. Teachers and parents who provide intentional opportunities for purposeful play help children learn and develop feelings of worthiness (Lozon & Brooks, 2019). For older students, the playfulness embedded in design thinking is as powerful in distance learning as it is face-to-face in schools. The pandemic of 2020 highlighted the distinctions that many adults draw between play and learning. But, this distinction limits understandings of powerful learning. Play is an essential component of learning—as demonstrated by the learning cycle model, design thinking, and many of the classroom practices described in this book.

The conventionally accepted goal of distance learning is to shepherd students through the curriculum when teachers and learners cannot occupy the same space. But, it is time to move beyond old conventions. When enduring learning is more important than coverage of material, applying learning theory and understandings of child development to this task becomes necessary. Distance learning, at its best, widens the circle of conversation. Teachers negotiate the academic syllabus not only with their students, but with other family members, as well.

In schools or in homes, imagine inviting students to push aside furniture to design and build geodesic domes out of rods of rolled newspaper or pieces of cardboard. Imagine the inquiries into shapes or discoveries of tessellations that may ensue. Imagine the studies of architecture it could prompt and the virtual tours to be taken of domes of many types found around the world. Imagine learning about Buckminster Fuller, known for popularizing the geodesic dome, and wondering why so few have heard of Walther Bauersfeld who built the first one. Through adult–child discussions and peer-to-peer exchanges, supported by online resources, classes can unfold as relevant whether in person or remotely.

Online learning platforms don't purport to be preferable to human interaction, collaboration, and investigations with physical materials, nor were they designed to be. But during social distancing mandates, they become the next best choice.

Notably, distance learning exacerbates concerns about equity. Not all students have the means or resources to access technology outside of school. Not all students have private spaces in which to study or adult supervision or mentoring. Not all students enjoy the security of safe housing and nutritious food. Many of today's schools are community schools, delivering meals to children in families without enough food; delivering specially prepared meals for children with unique health needs; providing books, packets of materials, and electronic tablets to families without technology; and paying for hotspots for families without Internet access. One of the lessons learned during the pandemic of 2020 is that the provision of these services to students and families was spotty. Provision for equitable access might ensure more equitable education under distance learning in the future. Many students are suffering, not only academically but also socially and emotionally.

During the onset of the pandemic of 2020, the national educational associations for each subject, museums big and small, and media organizations of all types expanded the range and access to instructional materials on their websites. A large number of them focused on collaboration, creativity, and problem solving, and also on social–emotional learning in response to students feeling lonely and frightened and isolated. We have learned that synchronous learning is important, not just because teachers can teach content and monitor progress face-to-face, but also because students crave connections with their teachers and also with their age peers: Seeing and speaking with their teachers provide the motivation to continue doing the asynchronous assignments they are given, and also give them the comfort of knowing that their teachers are safe and are thinking of them.

During school closings and hybrid education, the U.S. Department of Education waived federally mandated assessments, the College Board suspended administration of the SAT, Advanced Placement tests were shortened, and many states canceled state exams. An important lesson learned is that students can be educated without reliance on tests. Absent traditional means of assessment, Randi Weingarten, president of the American Federation of Teachers, said: "There are still meaningful ways teachers can help students sum up their academic progress and bring closure to this school year" (2020, para. 3). We agree. There are many meaningful ways to monitor student progress and assess learning.

Organizational changes such as the ones described above alter districts' procedural structures and cultural norms and communicate important messages about student learning throughout the system. One teacher with whom we worked often quoted Maya Angelou: "I did then what I knew how to do. Now that I know better, I do better."

PART III: STEPPING UP AND SPEAKING OUT	
Chapter 9 Shifting Norms and Structures	For transformations in teaching and learning to take root, organizational norms and structures must shift to facilitate acceptance of the changes within the system.
Chapter 10 Moving to the Next Level of Work	

Moving to the Next Level of Work

Student learning in school happens with and through the daily work of teachers. There are no shortcuts; there is no teacher proofing of schools. Curious and imaginative teachers empowered to be master learners serve as powerful guides for curious, imaginative students.

For today's schools to move to a next level of work, educators need to reimagine curricula, teaching methodologies, and assessment practices, and put the broader cognitive, emotional, and physical health of students, teachers, and community at the center of schools. Making changes around the margins is insufficient. This chapter calls for a transformation and presents a reimagining of schools in three parts: why, how, and for whom.

Students benefit when teachers have the freedom to do the right work—to ground curricula in disciplinary big ideas, to unpack it with students using transdisciplinary bigger ideas, to create lessons that actively seek students' voice and expand their points of view, to assess learning through multiple lenses, and to collaborate with colleagues when making impactful instructional decisions about students. Providing this latitude requires policymakers to cease replicating what doesn't work, rescind unproductive laws and regulations, and focus their efforts on the body of well-respected and vetted research that supports what is known about student learning (Darling-Hammond et al., 2007). To do otherwise simply makes no sense.

During the global health pandemic, a new approach to teaching and learning was created and implemented. The creators and implementers were teachers, many of whom had limited prior experience with the technology-based platforms on which the new structures were built. As discussed at the end of the previous chapter, some important lessons were learned, one of which is that much of what is considered standard operating procedure—seat time, paced schedules, testing, and grading, for example—although linked to our historical conception of schooling may not be necessary, and certainly isn't fundamental to learning. Millions of children throughout the nation, given assignments by their teachers and assisted to varying degrees by their parents, continued to learn at home without being tested or graded. They regulated themselves.

When given the opportunity, students regulate themselves in school as well. Emerging from the pandemic, and with the authority of cognitive science, neuroscience, and classroom research behind them, educators can reject the push toward standardization and reimagine schooling.

Well known for his thinking about creativity, innovation, and the development of human potential, Sir Ken Robinson wrote:

> The fact is that given the challenges we face, education doesn't need to be reformed—it needs to be transformed. The key to this transformation is not to standardize education, but to personalize it, to build achievement on discovering the individual talents of each child, to put students in an environment where they want to learn and where they can naturally discover their true passions. (2009, p. 283)

WHY

Teaching to the test has defined the nation's educational landscape for years (Kohn, 2000). Standardization, usually driven by and monitored through testing, limits student engagement and conflates learning with memorization. History has taught us that students frequently forget what they memorize, often quickly. They also disengage from activities without a purpose recognizable to them. Testing and standardization certainly diminish students' natural curiosity (Zhao, 2012).

The 10-year implementation of the English Language Arts Common Core Standards, for example, which were designed to increase literacy, has actually witnessed a decrease in literacy (Barnum, 2019), while simultaneously imposing a costly, long, and harmful list of meaningless activities on students that have resulted in disaffected readers (Schmoker, 2020). Students don't forget what is meaningful. They remember the ideas that they build, and they deserve schools that help them build those ideas.

Compare the empowering principles of constructivist learning with the constricting beliefs and punitive practices of the federal education laws that have dominated the past 3 decades. These federal regulations use threats and sanctions to drive school improvement based on test score audits. It hasn't worked. No one who understands human learning would have predicted it would.

There are inherent challenges in finding new solutions to persistent dilemmas. However, it is clear that testing, as an engine for or metric of school improvement, has failed. James Popham (1999), noted expert on testing, wrote: "Employing standardized achievement tests to ascertain educational quality is like measuring temperature with a tablespoon" (para 18).

Research over many years shows that biases are built into the vast majority of standardized tests, almost all of which advantage certain groups of students and disadvantage others—by wealth, race, language, culture, development, disability (Kohn, 2000; Popham, 2003; Ravitch, 2010) and more recently, by facility with and access to technology. Several years ago, as the PARCC and SBAC exams were being developed and rolled out, there was much hullabaloo about them—purportedly these tests would assess students' critical thinking abilities, knowledge bases and skills, and would reduce the extent to which students' test scores are related to family wealth. Quickly it became apparent that these new tests accomplished none of these goals well, and the majority of the 48 states that initially signed on to administer them have subsequently jettisoned them. Not surprisingly, students' zip codes still predict test scores with remarkable accuracy. Tienken (2017) writes, "Standardized test results tell us more about the community in which a student lives than the amount the student has learned or the academic, social and emotional growth of the student during a school year" (para. 22).

Even more disturbing, standardized tests promote the ranking, sorting, and classifying of students, ironically perpetuating the very same inequities they claim to address. Based on a score obtained on one test on one day students are labeled as "remedial," "general education," or "advanced." We know better and our students deserve better, and continued participation in these discriminatory practices makes us all complicitous. We are participating in a perversion damaging to great numbers of students, the teachers who educate them, and the communities they serve. It's time to push back against this charade. This push won't be easy—it will require courage and hard work, but the potential rewards for students make the effort imperative.

Human learning theory cuts across eras, cultures, races, genders, and socioeconomics, provides a different window into school quality, and offers a new entry point. It is time to align our work with research on learning and development and professionalize the work of teachers (Berliner, 2017). It is time to unify the science of learning with the art of teaching.

Many educators with whom we have spoken are ready for this change. They see the discrepancies between what test scores purport to indicate and what student work actually demonstrates, and want a different, more student-centered lens through which they can approach their work with students and document learning. In response to the burgeoning reliance on test scores as proxies for school quality, Ravitch (2010) lamented: "I saw my hopes for better education turn into a measurement strategy that had no underlying educational vision at all. Eventually I realized that the new reforms had everything to do with structural changes and accountability, and nothing at all to do with the substance of learning" (p. 16). It's time to focus on the substance of learning.

Education is the cornerstone of free-thinking peoples—without it, doors remain closed, and, with it, possibilities appear. Across the world, 200 million young people leave school without the skills they need to thrive, and an estimated 775 million adults, 64% of whom are women, lack rudimentary reading and writing skills (UNESCO, 2013). Thirty percent of countries worldwide still do not have gender parity in primary school, and 50% do not have it in secondary school (Costin, 2017).

Although more children now than ever are enrolled in schools, an estimated 250 million children around the globe cannot read, write, or count, "whether they have been to school or not" (UNESCO, 2013, p. 2). The number is staggering, but the phrase "whether they have been to school or not" is equally staggering and raises the question: If some of these children have been in schools, what have they been doing? Going to school should make a difference. How success is defined matters. Defining success as a function of students' compliance, behavior, and scores on tests is decidedly different than defining success through the lens of self-regulation and the construction and application of meaningful knowledge. The former is neat and easily amenable to standard forms of assessing and grading, while the latter is messy, complex, and defies the assignment of one simple letter or numerical grade.

HOW

Determining school quality is not easy work, and the factors that affect school quality are complicated and interrelated. Figure 10.1 represents a summary of 10 complex and interrelated changes suggested throughout the book.

Figure 10.1. Quality School Actions

- Place the search for meaning at the center of educative practice.
- Implement curricula that encourage the search for meaning through design challenges and big ideas.
- Use the frameworks underpinning the national standards as intellectual tools in planning lessons.
- Seek and value student voice by encouraging expression of points of view.
- Recognize the productive role of error in learning.
- Align institutional norms and structures with desired changes in curriculum and instruction.
- Identify outcomes worthy of student and teacher time, and target curriculum and instructional practice toward them.
- Identify and capture evidence related to worthy outcomes.
- Use multiple measures to assess student learning.
- Confront and alter practices that interfere with social justice, equity, and access.

Teaching requires a pedagogical and disciplinary knowledge base and the autonomy to make independent, time-sensitive decisions. Teachers must be decisionmakers more than implementers of others' decisions, creators and negotiators of curriculum more than disseminators of information, and advocates for each student's education rather than compliance officers. Districts accepting that students are natural constructors of knowledge must hire and support teachers who see themselves as natural constructors of knowledge themselves.

Think about walking a curved street from a different direction. Buildings that were always there are seen for the first time from a new perspective. Trees unnoticed before now loom large. The views change dramatically, while the street, still the same, looks different from a different perspective. Teaching in schools with new perspectives on how people learn is like walking that curved street in a different way.

FOR WHOM

Ben is a kindergartener with passionate and poetic interests in the natural world. His class went on a field trip to a nearby farm to pick strawberries. Upon returning to school, he met the principal's secretary in the hall, who asked if he enjoyed the trip. He replied: "It was a red heaven." This is Ben. He speaks in metaphors and dances to the beat of his own drummer. In a school with very informally dressed teachers and students, Ben enjoys wearing a blazer and tie every day. He carries old textbooks for reading material wherever he goes. His relationships with his peers are complicated. He would rather read his books.

Ben's independent study of volcanoes is so deep that a 3rd-grade teacher asked if he might like to make a presentation to her class. He did, mesmerizing the 3rd-graders with his articulate explanations, charts, and photos. At the end, he asked if there were any questions. One 3rd-grader raised her hand and asked: "How do we know that there's not a volcano under us right now?" Ben, who hadn't considered that possibility, thought for a moment and said: "There couldn't be. If a volcano was below us, the ground would be very hot and the grass would turn brown. It's not brown. As long as the grass stays green, I think we're safe." Ben's ability to predict safety and his understanding of the geology of the region may not be fully accurate, but his wonderments and logic are inspirational. Ben needs schools that will nurture him as he grows, not tell him he is unable to pursue his interests and seek to have him conform to rules that will stunt his curiosity.

Ben and all his classmates deserve the chance to wonder and consider. Some wondering and considering brings us to intellectual dead ends. When that happens, we plan, analyze, synthesize, and find out, and we *think* about what we are planning, analyzing, synthesizing, and finding out, and we *talk* about and *listen* to each other's thinking. In other words, we reflect on what and how we think, and we learn.

Schools often organize classrooms to expect and require immediate success when so many other aspects of our lives tell us that error is a critical part of the learning process, and a critical component of eventual success. Teachers who encourage students to investigate big ideas, meaningful and relevant issues, and interesting phenomena help students see that exploring ideas matters. These are the educators we need.

Working on challenges that use our unique talents, with focus, involvement, and commitment, generates "flow," a concept researched and made popular by the noted psychologist Mihaly Csikszentmihalyi (1990). Flow is a mental state of well-being that arises when one is completely immersed in creative engagement. Bailey, a 4th-grader leaving her classroom after having spent hours immersed in designing a pulley system to rescue a toy kitten from a tunnel, looked up at Ms. Smith and said: "This has been the best day of my life."

Ms. Smith and her colleagues are creating the schools that Ben and Bailey and their classmates need, and the schools she and her colleagues need—schools that offer students many "best days of their lives," that enable teachers and students to seek understanding, that encourage them to be informed, caring, ethical citizens of the world.

We close with the words of Paolo Friere:

> Teacher preparation should go beyond the technical preparation of teachers and be rooted in the ethical formation both of selves and of history. . . . I am speaking of a universal human ethic, an ethic that is not afraid to condemn . . . the manipulation that makes a rumor into truth and truth into a mere rumor. To condemn the fabrication of illusions, in which the unprepared become hopelessly trapped and the weak and the defenseless are destroyed. . . . For the sake of this ethic, which is inseparable from educative practice, we should struggle, whether our work is with children, youth, or adults. (1998, p. 23)

Friere urges openness to an ethic of truth, recognizes it as a struggle, and situates this ethic squarely in the lap of education. In schools, commitment to this ethic is how we, as individuals, come to understand our worlds, and how we, as an educational community, uncover collective paths toward creating and sustaining a democratic society. Educators have enormous influence on the development of their students' thinking. That influence can be ignored or misused, or it can be applied generatively in service to learning. All students have something to contribute to our global community, and all teachers, with openness, can help them realize their contributions. These are the schools we need. This is our next level of work. This is where the science of learning intersects with the art of teaching.

PART III: STEPPING UP AND SPEAKING OUT	
Chapter 9 Shifting Norms and Structures	For transformations in teaching and learning to take root, organizational norms and structures must shift to facilitate acceptance of the changes within the system.
Chapter 10 Moving to the Next Level of Work	Because changes around the margins are insufficient, transformative educators rethink curricula, instruction, and assessment and place the broader cognitive, emotional, and physical well-being of students, teachers, and community at the center of schools.

References

Ackermann, E. (2001). *Piaget's constructivism, Papert's constructionism: What's the difference?* MIT Media Lab. https://learning.media.mit.edu/content/publications /EA.Piaget%20_%20Papert.pdf

Adair, J. K., Colegrove, K. S.-S., & McManus, M. E. (2017, Fall). How the word gap argument negatively impacts young children of Latinx immigrants' conceptualizations of learning. *Harvard Educational Review.* Harvard Education Publishing Group.

American Library Association. (2018). *Standards framework for learners.* American Association of School Librarians.

Arlin, P. K. (1975). Cognitive development in adulthood: A fifth stage? *Developmental Psychology, 11*(5), 602–606.

Ashton-Warner, S. (1986). *Teacher.* Simon & Schuster. (Original work published 1963)

Atkin, J. M., & Karplus, R. (1962). Discovery or invention. *The Science Teacher, 29*(2), 121–143.

Ball, D. L., & Forzani, F. M. (2010, December/2011, January). Teaching skillful teaching. *Educational Leadership, 68*(4), 40–45.

Barnum, M. (2019, April 12). Nearly a decade later, did the Common Core work? New research offers clues. *Chalkbeat.*

Berliner, D. C. (2017, March 2). The purported failure of America's schools, and ways to make them better. *Equity Alliance Blog.*

Bigelow, B. (2020). *Zinn education project.* https://www.zinnedproject.org/author -bios/bill-bigelow

Bigelow, B., & Swinehart, T. (Eds.). (2014). *A people's curriculum for the Earth.* Rethinking School.

Blair, C., & Razza, R. P. (2007). Relating effortful control, executive function, and false belief understanding to emerging math and literacy ability in kindergarten. *Child Development, 78*(2), 647–663.

Blakemore, S.-J. (2018). *Inventing ourselves: The secret life of the teenage brain.* Public Affairs.

Brooks, J. G. (2002). *Schooling for life, reclaiming the essence of learning.* Association for Supervision and Curriculum Development.

Brooks, J. G. (2011). *Big science for growing minds: Constructivist classrooms for young thinkers.* Teachers College Press.

Brooks, J. G., & Brooks, M. G. (1999). *In search of understanding: The case for constructivist classrooms.* Association for Supervision and Curriculum Development.

Brooks, J. G., & Caliendo, J. (2012, Spring). STEM Studio: Where teaching is learning and learning is research. *Hofstra Horizons*. Hofstra University.

Brooks, M. G., Fusco, E., & Grennon, J. (1983). Cognitive levels matching. *Educational Leadership*. Association for Supervision and Curriculum Development.

Brown, B. (2010, June). *Brené Brown: The power of vulnerability* [Video File]. https://www.ted.com/talks/brene_brown_the_power_of_vulnerability?fbclid=IwAR20WgWeI-D2mU37HJPaJW1Nze2_Kd4y4O08UH12o8VcUtfKEdHshMBShOI#t-63856

Bruner, J. (1960). *The process of education*. The President and Fellows of Harvard College.

Bruner, J. (1971). *The relevance of education*. Norton.

Caliendo, J., & Brooks, J. G. (2013). [Outcome evaluation of STEM studio program on elementary and secondary student performance]. Hofstra University. Unpublished raw data.

CAST (Center for Applied Special Technology). (2018). *Universal design for learning guidelines (Version 2.2)*. http://udlguidelines.cast.org

Centers for Disease Control and Prevention. (2017a). *School health index: A self-assessment and planning guide, elementary school version*.

Centers for Disease Control and Prevention. (2017b). *School health index: A self-assessment and planning guide, middle school/high school version*.

Centers for Disease Control and Prevention & Association for Supervision and Curriculum Development. (2014). *Whole school, whole community, whole child (WSCC) model*. https://www.cdc.gov/healthyschools/wscc/index.htm

Chomsky, N. (1977). *Language and responsibility*. Pantheon Books.

Chomsky, N. (2006). *Language and mind* (3rd ed.). Cambridge University Press.

Clark, D. B., & Linn, M. C. (2013). The knowledge integration perspective: Connections across research and education. In S. Vosniadou (Ed.), *International handbook of research on conceptual change*. Routledge. https://doi.org/10.4324/9780203154472

Copple, C., Sigel, I., & Saunders, R. (1984). *Educating the young thinker*. D. Van Nostrand.

Costin, C. (2017, August 3). What is the role of teachers in preparing future generations? In Brooking Institute (Ed.), *Meaningful education in times of uncertainty: A collection of essays from the Center for Universal Education*. https://www.brookings.edu/opinions/what-is-the-role-of-teachers-in-preparing-future-generations

Counsell, S. L., Escalada, L., Geiken, R., Sander, M., Uhlenberg, J., Van Meeteren, B., Yoshizawa, S., & Zan, B. (2015). *STEM learning with young children: Inquiry teaching with ramps and pathways*. Teachers College Press.

Csikszentmihalyi, M. (1990). *Flow: The psychology of optimal experience*. Harper & Row.

Darling-Hammond, L., Barron, B., Pearson, P. D., Schoenfeld, A. H., Stage, E. K., Zimmerman, T. D., Cervetti, G. N., & Tilson, J. L. (2008). *Powerful learning: What we know about teaching for understanding*. Jossey-Bass.

Davis, B. (2018). Here are 6 big ideas that gripped the art world in 2018: From 'platform capitalism' to 'chthulucene.' *ArtNet News*. https://news.artnet.com/art-world/6-big-ideas-in-art-2018-1422307

Delbert, C. (2019, December 6). Mathematician finds easier way to solve quadratic equations. *Popular Mechanics*. https://www.popularmechanics.com/science/math/a30152083/solve-quadratic-equations

Dennick, R. (2016). Constructivism: Reflections on twenty five years teaching the constructivist approach in medical education. *International Journal of Medical Education*, 7, 200–205. http://doi.org/10.5116/ijme.5763.de11

DeRuy, E. (2016, May 20). Does mindfulness actually work in schools? *The Atlantic (online)*.

DeVries, R., & Sales, C. (2010). *Ramps and pathways: A constructivist approach to physics with young children*. The National Association for the Education of Young Children.

DeVries, R., & Zan, B. (2012). *Moral classrooms, moral children: Creating a constructivist atmosphere in early childhood education*. Teachers College Press.

Dewey, J. (1900). *The school and society*. University of Chicago Press.

Dewey, J. (1997). *Experience and education*. Simon & Schuster. (Original work published 1938)

Dolan, R. P., & Hall, T. E. (2001). Universal design for learning: Implications for large-scale assessment. *IDA Perspectives*, 27(4), 22–25.

Driver, R., Squires, A., Rushworth, P., & Wood-Robinson, V. (1994). *Making sense of secondary science*. Routledge.

Duckworth, E. (1972). The having of wonderful ideas. *Harvard Education Review*, 42(2), 217–231.

Duckworth, E. (2006). *The having of wonderful ideas and other essays on teaching and learning*. Teachers College Press.

Duke, N. K., & Pearson, P. D. (2002). Effective practices for developing reading comprehension. In A. E. Farstrup & S. J. Samuels (Eds.), *What research has to say about reading instruction* (3rd ed.). International Reading Association.

Dweck, C. S. (2007). *Mindset: The new psychology of success*. Ballantine Books.

Edmonds, D., & Warburton, N. (Eds.). (2016). *Big ideas in social science*. Sage.

Edwards, C., Gandini, L., & Forman, G. (Eds.). (1998). *Hundred languages of children: The Reggio Emilia approach to early childhood education* (2nd ed.). Elsevier Science.

Elkind, D. (1978). *The child's reality: Three developmental themes*. Erlbaum.

Elkind, D. (2001). *The hurried child: Growing up too fast too soon*. Perseus. (Original work published 1981)

Elmore, R. F. (2005). Agency, reciprocity, and accountability in democratic education. In S. Furhman & M. Lazerson (Eds.), *The public schools*. Oxford University Press.

Epstein, H. R. (1978). Growth spurts during brain development: Implications for educational policy and practice. In J. S. Chall & A. F. Mirsky (Eds.), *NSSE yearbook education and the brain* (pp. 343–370). University of Chicago Press.

Ernst, K., & Ryan, S. (2014). *Success from the start: Your first years teaching elementary mathematics*. National Council of Teachers of Mathematics.

Etkina, E., & Mestra, J. P. (2004, August 5–9). Implications of learning research for teaching science to non-science majors. *SENCER Summer Institute*. Santa Clara University.

Feuerstein, R., Feuerstein, R. S., Falik, L. H., (2010). *Beyond smarter: Mediated learning and the brain's capacity for change.* Teachers College Press.

Feuerstein, R., Feuerstein, R. S., Falik, L. H., & Rand, Y. (2002). *Dynamic assessments of cognitive modifiability.* ICELP Press. (Original work published 1979)

Fischer, K. W. (2009). *Mind, brain, and education: Building a scientific groundwork for learning and teaching.* International Mind, Brain, and Education Society and Wiley Periodicals, 3(1).

Fitzsimmons, R. (2007a, November 15). Mathematics in the museum. *Welcome booklet, Ringling Museum of Art.* The State Art Museum of Florida.

Fitzsimmons, R. (2007b, November 15). Metal and the effects of weather. *Welcome booklet, Ringling Museum of Art.* The State Art Museum of Florida.

Flook, L., Smalley, S. L., Kitil, M. J., Kaiser-Greenland, S., Locke, J., Ishijima, E., & Kasari, C. (2010). Mindful awareness practices on executive functions in elementary school. *Children Journal of Applied School Psychology, 26*(2), 70–95.

Forman, G., & Pufall, P. B. (Eds.). (1988). *Constructivism in the computer age.* Erlbaum.

Fosnot, C. T. (1993). Rethinking science education: A defense of Piagetian constructivism. *Journal for Research in Science Education, 30*(9), 1189–1201.

Fosnot, C. T. (1996, 2005). *Constructivism: Theory, perspectives, and practice.* Teachers College Press.

Fosnot, C. T., & Dolk, M. (2001). *Young mathematicians at work: Constructing number sense, addition and subtraction.* Heinemann.

Friere, P. (1998). *Pedagogy of freedom.* Rowman & Littlefield. (Original work published 1996)

Friere, P. (2000). *Pedagogy of the oppressed.* Bloomsbury. (Original work published 1970)

Fromberg, D., & Bergen, D. (Eds.). (2015). *Play from birth to 12: Contexts, perspectives, and meanings* (2nd ed.). Routledge.

Fullan, M. (2001). *Leading in a culture of change.* Wiley.

Fullan, M. (2003). *The moral imperative of school leadership.* Corwin Press.

Fullan, M. (2011). *Change leader.* Wiley.

Fullan, M., Quinn, J., & McEachen, J. (2018). *Deep learning: Engage the world Change the world.* Corwin Press and Ontario Principals' Council.

Furth, H. G., & Wachs, H. (1975). *Thinking goes to school: Piaget's theory in practice.* Oxford University Press.

Gallant, S. N. (2016, February). Mindfulness meditation practice and executive functioning: Breaking down the benefit. *Consciousness and Cognition, 40,* 116–130. Elsevier.

Gamse, B. C., Jacob, R. T., Horst, M., Boulay, B., & Unlu, F. (2008). *Reading first impact study: Final report.* NCEE 2009-4038. National Center for Education Evaluation and Regional Assistance. Institute of Education Sciences, U.S. Department of Education.

Gardner, H. (1983). *Frames of mind: The theory of multiple intelligences.* Basic Books.

Gardner, H. (1991). *The unschooled mind: How children think and how schools should teach.* Basic Books.

Gilligan, C. (1982). *In a different voice.* Erlbaum.

Giroux, H. (2011). *On critical pedagogy*. Bloomsbury Academic.

Glasser, W. (1998). *The quality school*. HarperPerennial. (Original work published 1990)

Glatthorn, A. (2004). *Developing a quality curriculum*. Waveland Press.

Gleason, J. B., & Ratner, N. B. (2013). *Development of language* (8th ed.). Pearson.

Goodman, Y., & Martens, P. (2007). *Critical issues in early literacy*. Routledge.

Guvenir, C., & Bagli, H. H. (2019). The potentials of learning object design in design thinking learning. *Markets, Globalization & Development Review, 4*(2), Article 3. doi:10.23860/MGDR-2019-04-02-03. Available at https://digitalcommons.uri .edu/mgdr/vol4/iss2/3https://digitalcommons.uri.edu/mgdr/vol4/ iss2/3

Harlan, W. (Ed.), with Bell, D., Devés, R., Dyasi, H., Fernández de la Garza, G., Léna, P., Millar, R., Reiss, M., Rowell, P., & Yu, W. (2015). *Working with big ideas of science education*. Science Education Programme of the Interacademic Partnership (IAP).

Hebb, D. O. (1949). *The organization of behavior: A neuropsychological theory*. Psychology Press.

Herold, B. (2016, April 11). *The maker movement in k-12 education: A guide to emerging research*. http://blogs.edweek.org/edweek/DigitalEducation/2016/04 /maker_movement_in_k-12_education_research.html

Jacobs, H. H., & Alcock, M. H. (2018). *Bold moves*. Association for Supervision and Curriculum Development.

Johnson, S. M. (2005). Working in schools. In S. Fuhrman & M. Lazerson (Eds.), *The public schools*. Oxford University Press.

Jones, H., Black, B., Green, J., Langton, P., Rutherford, S., Scott, J., & Brown, S. (2014). Indications of knowledge retention in the transition to higher education. *Journal of Biological Education, 1*. doi:10.1080/00219266.2014.926960

Kabat-Zinn, J. (2013). *Full catastrophe living*. Bantam.

Kallick, B., & Zmuda, A. (2017). *Students at the center: Personalized learning with habits of mind*. Association for Supervision and Curriculum Development.

Kamii, C. (1993). *Young children reinvent arithmetic: Implications of Piaget's theory*. Teachers College Press.

Kamii, C. (2011). Place value: An explanation of its difficulty and educational implications for the primary grades. *Journal of Research in Childhood Education, 1*(2), 75–86.

Kamii, C., & DeVries, R. (1993). *Physical knowledge in preschool education: Implications of Piaget's theory*. Teachers College Press.

Kirp, D. L. (2017, June 11). End the curse of remedial math. *Sunday Review* (p. 6). New York Times.

Kohlberg, L. (1981). *The philosophy of moral development*. Harper & Row.

Kohn, A. (1993). *Punished by rewards: The trouble with gold stars, incentive plan, A's, praise, and other bribes*. Houghton Mifflin.

Kohn, A. (2000). *The case against standardized testing: Raising the scores, ruining the schools*. Heinemann.

Konan, D. E., & Morgan, J. M. (2016). *Climate change science and economics*. National Center for Science and Civic Engagement. http://ncsce.net/climate-change -science-and-economics

Kozol, J. (1967). *Death at an early age*. Houghton Mifflin.

Kurlansky, M. (2003). *Salt: A world history*. Penguin Books.

Labinowicz, E. (1980). *The Piaget primer: Thinking, teaching, learning.* Addison-Wesley.

Lawson, A. E., & Karplus, R. (2002). The learning cycle. In R. G. Fuller (Eds.), *A love of discovery: Innovations in science education and technology.* Springer.

Learner-Centered Principles Work Group of the American Psychological Association's Board of Educational Affairs. (1997, November [APA]). *Learner-centered psychological principles: A framework for school reform and redesign.* American Psychological Association. https://www.apa.org/ed/governance/bea/learner -centered.pdf

Linn, M. C. (1983). Content, context, and process in adolescent reasoning. *Journal of Early Adolescence, 3,* 63–82.

Linn, M. C. (2006). The knowledge integration perspective on learning and instruction. In R. Sawyer (Ed.), *The Cambridge handbook of the learning sciences.* Cambridge University Press.

Louv, R. (2008). *Last child in the woods: Saving our children from nature-deficit disorder.* Algonquin Books.

Louv, R. (2012). *The nature principle: Reconnecting with life in a virtual age.* Algonquin Books.

Lozon, C., & Brooks, J. G. (2019, October). The potential of purposeful play: Using the lens and language of crosscutting concepts to enhance the science and engineering practices of play. *International Journal of the Whole Child. Tennessee Association for Childhood Education International, 4*(2). ISSN 2474-297X

Luka, I. (2014). Design thinking in pedagogy. *Journal of Education, Culture and Society, 2,* 63–74.

Ma, L. (1999). *Knowing and teaching elementary mathematics.* Studies in Mathematical Thinking Series. Routledge.

Mahn, H. (1999). Vygotsky's methodological contribution to sociocultural theory. *Remedial and Special Education, 20*(6), 341–351. doi:10.1177/074193259902 000607

Mann, H. (1852). *The common school journal.* Marsh, Capen, Lyon, & Webb.

Martin-Kniep, G. (2014, July 1). *Performance based assessment in schools.* Lecture for Tri-State Consortium, Rye, NY.

Martinelli, K. (2019, August 15). *Can climbing trees replace preparing for tests?* New York Times. https://parenting.nytimes.com/preschooler/forest-school?fbclid=Iw AR3e8URcVFofYsWOJuV5Kw1StXAeSXvBq2TRNEPtJsxj2kjIxuKJAdyZydk

Mathews, J. (1998). *What's wrong (and right) with America's best public high schools.* Crown.

Maxwell, J. C. (2007). *Failing forward: Turning mistakes into stepping stones for success.* Thomas Nelson.

McKay, R., & Teale, W. H. (2015). *Not this but that: No more teaching a letter a week.* Heinemann.

McLaughlin, M. W. (1976, February). Implementation as mutual adaptation: Change in classroom organization. *Teachers College Record, 77*(3), 339–351.

Mehta, J., & Fine, S. (2019a). *In search of deeper learning: The quest to remake the American high school.* Harvard University Press.

Mehta, J., & Fine, S. (2019b, March 31). High school doesn't have to be boring. *New York Times.* https://www.nytimes.com/2019/03/30/opinion/sunday/fix -high-school-education.html

Merrow, J. (2019, November 1). Montessori, Dewey, & Aristotle respond to NAEP decline. *The Merrow Report.* themerrowreport.com/2019/11

Mitchell, L. S. (1916). *Bureau of educational experiments in New York.* Vintage.

Museum of Science Boston. (2017). *Engineering is elementary: Design process.* http://www.eie.org/overview/engineering-design-process

Nair, P. (2014). *Blueprint for tomorrow: Redesigning schools for student-centered learning.* Harvard Education Press.

Nair, P., Fielding, R., & Lackney, J. (2009). *The language of school design: Design patterns for 21st century schools.* DesignShare.com.

NASA Earth Observatory. (2017). *Coal vs. banana: A two-minute explanation of the carbon cycle.* https://www.youtube.com/watch?v=uStoBFtjy8U

National Coalition for Core Arts Standards. (2015). *National core arts standards.* State Education Agency Directors of Arts Education.

National Council for the Social Studies. (2010). *National curriculum standards for social studies.*

National Council of Teachers of English (2018, October 25). *Beliefs for integrating technology into the English language arts classroom.* https://ncte.org/statement/beliefs-technology-preparation-english-teachers

National Council of Teachers of English. (2019). *NCTE framework for 21st century curriculum and assessment.*

National Governors Association Center for Best Practices and Council of Chief State School Officers. (2010). *Common core state standards for mathematics (CC-SSM).* http://www.corestandards.org/wp-content/uploads/Math_Standards.pdf

National Oceanic and Atmospheric Administration (NOAA). (2017). *Per-capita consumption.* https://www.st.nmfs.noaa.gov/st1/fus/fus04/08_perita2004.pdf

National Research Council (NRC). (2000). *How people learn: Brain, mind, experience, and school: Expanded edition.* The National Academies Press. https://doi.org/10.17226/9853

National Research Council (NRC). (2005). *How students learn: History, mathematics, and science in the classroom.* The National Academies Press. https://doi.org/10.17226/10126

National Standards Collaborative Board. (2015). *World-readiness standards for learning languages* (4th ed).

Newman, D., Griffin, P., & Cole, M. (1989). *The construction zone: Working for cognitive change in school.* Cambridge University Press.

NGSS Lead States. (2013). *Next generation science standards: For states, by states.* The National Academies Press.

Noddings, N. L. (1995). *Philosophy of education.* Dimensions of Philosophy Series. Westview Press.

NSTA Press Picture Perfect Science Teaching Channel. (2019). *Simulating an oil spill to understand environmental impact.* https://ngss.nsta.org/Resource.aspx?ResourceID=65

Oakes, J. (2005). *Keeping track: How schools structure inequality.* Yale University Press.

Ohanian, S. (1999). *One size fits few: The folly of educational standards.* Heinemann.

Papert, S. (1965). Introduction to Warren S. McCulloch. *Embodiments of mind.* MIT Press. http://www.papert.org/articles/embodiments.html

Papert, S. (1980). *Mindstorms: Children, computers and powerful ideas* (2nd ed.). Basic Books.

Papert, S. (1988). The conservation of Piaget: The computer as grist for the constructivist mill. In G. Forman & P. B. Pufall (Eds.), *Constructivism in the computer age*. Erlbaum.

Piaget, J. (1923). *The language and thought of the child*. Routledge.

Piaget, J. (1952). *The origins of intelligence in children*. International Universities Press.

Piaget, J. (1977). *The development of thought: Equilibration of cognitive structures*. Basil Blackwell.

Piaget, J. (1985). *Equilibration of cognitive structures: The central problem of intellectual development*. University of Chicago Press. (Original work published 1977)

Piaget, J., & Inhelder, B. (1971). *The psychology of the child*. Basic Books.

Picasso, P. (1923), quoted in Barr, A. H., Jr. (1946). *Picasso: Fifty years of his art*. Quote on p. 270, col. 1. The Museum of Modern Art.

Piercy, M. (1982). *Circles on the Water: Selected Poems of Marge Piercy*. Knopf.

Pisha, B., & Coyne, P., (2001). Smart from the start: The promise of universal design for learning. *Remedial and Special Education, 22*(4), 197–203.

Plattner, H., Meinel, C., & Leifer, L. (Eds.). (2016). *Design thinking research: Making design thinking foundational*. Springer.

Popham, W. J. (1999). Why standardized test scores don't measure educational quality. *Educational Leadership, 56*(6), 8–15.

Popham, W. J. (2003). *Teach better, test better*. Association for Supervision and Curriculum Development.

Postman, N. (1995). *The end of education*. Vintage Books.

Pozuelos, J. P., & Malinowski, P. (2019). Short-term mindful breath awareness training improves inhibitory control and response monitoring. *Progress in Brain Research, 244*, 137–163.

Pulaski, M. A. S. (1980). *Understanding Piaget*. Harper & Row.

Quartz, S. R., & Sejnowski, T. J. (1997). The neural basis of cognitive development: A constructivist manifesto. *Behavioral and Brain Science, 20*(4), 537–596.

Radcliffe, S. (Ed.). (2017). *Oxford essential quotations* (5th ed.). Oxford University Press. Online Version: 2017eISBN: 9780191843730.

Ramachandran, V. S. (2011). *The tell-tale brain: Unlocking the mysteries of human nature*. Heinemann.

Rand, G. (1994). *Prince William*. Square Fish.

Ravitch, D. (2010). *The death and life of the great American school system: How testing and choice are undermining education*. Basic Books.

Rawls, W. (1961). *Where the red fern grows*. Doubleday.

Rhinow, A., Noweski, C., & Meinel, C. (2012). *Transforming constructivist learning into action: Design thinking in education*. https://www.researchgate.net/publication/332343908_Transforming_Constructivist_Learning_into_Action_Design_Thinking_in_education

Robinson, K. (2009). *The element: How finding your passion changes everything*. Penguin Books.

Roser, M., & Ortiz-Ospina, E. (2017). *World population growth*. OurWorldInData.org. https://ourworldindata.org/world-population-growth

Rushkoff, D. (2012, November 13). *Code literacy: A 21st-century requirement*. https://www.edutopia.org/blog/code-literacy-21st-century-requirement-douglas-rushkoff

Rushton, S., & Larkin, E. (2001). Shaping the learning environment: Connecting developmentally appropriate practices to brain research. *Early Childhood Education Journal, 29,* 25–33. https://doi.org/10.1023/A:1011304805899

Scheer, A., Noweski, C., & Meinel, C. (2012). Transforming constructivist learning into action: Design thinking in education. *Design and Technology Education Journal, 17*(3), 8–19.

Schifter, D. (2001). Learning to see the invisible: What skills and knowledge are needed to engage with students' mathematical ideas? In T. Wood, B. S. Nelson, & J. Warfield (Eds.). *Beyond classroom pedagogy: Teaching elementary school mathematics* (pp. 109–134). Erlbaum.

Schmoker, M. (2020, February). Radical reset: The case for minimalist literacy standards. *Educational Leadership, 77*(5), 44–50.

Shaul, S. M., & Schwartz, M. (2014). The role of the executive functions in school readiness among preschool-age children. *Reading and Writing, 27*(4), 749–768.

Siegel, D. (2010). *The mindful therapist: A clinician's guide to mindsight and neural integration.* Norton.

Simonton, D. K. (1994). *Greatness: Who makes history and why.* Guilford.

Slavin, R. E., Lake, C., Hanley, P., & Thurston, A. (2014). Experimental evaluations of elementary science programs: A best-evidence synthesis. *Journal of Research in Science Teaching, 51*(7), 870–901.

Smith, T. W., & Colby, S. A. (2007, May/June). Teaching for deep learning. *The Clearing House, 80*(5), 205–210.

Sobel, D. (2013). *Place-based education: Connecting classroom and community.* Orion.

Steffe, L. P., Hirstein, J., & Spikes, C. (1976). Quantitative comparison and class inclusion as readiness variables for learning first grade arithmetic content. *PMDC Technical Report No. 9,* Project for Mathematical Development of Children, Tallahassee. ERIC database (ED144808).

Steffe L. P., & Ulrich, C. (2014). Constructivist teaching experiment. In S. Lerman (Ed.), *Encyclopedia of mathematics education.* Springer.

Steinbeck, J. (1937). *Of mice and men.* Covivi Freide.

Stornaiuolo, A., & Nichols, P. (2016). *Making publics: The iterative design of high school makerspaces. American Educational Research Association.*

Sutcliffe, K. M., Vogus, T. J., & Dane, E. (2016). Mindfulness in organizations: A cross-level review. *Annual Review of Organizational Psychology and Organizational Behavior, 3,* 55–81. doi:10.1146/annurev-orgpsych-041015-062531

Tai, R. H., Liu, C. Q., Maltese, A. V., & Fan, X. (2006). Planning early for careers in science. *Science, 312*(5777), 1143–1144.

Tang, Y., Hölzel, B., & Posner, M. (2015). The neuroscience of mindfulness meditation. *Nature Reviews Neuroscience, 16,* 213–225. https://doi.org/10.1038/nrn3916

Teale, W. H., Paciga, K. A., & Hoffman, J. L. (2007). Beginning reading instruction in urban schools: The curriculum gap ensures a continuing achievement gap. *The Reading Teacher, 61*(4), 344–348.

Thompson-Grove, G. (2000, November). *ATLAS, learning from student work. National School Reform Faculty.* https://www.nsrfharmony.org/wp-content/uploads/2017/10/atlas_lfsw_0.pdf

Thornburg, D. (2013). *From the campfire to the holodeck: Creating engaging and powerful 21st century learning environments.* Jossey-Bass.

Tienken, C. (2017, July 5). Students' test scores tell us more about the community than what they know. *The Conversation.* https://theconversation.com/students-test-scores-tell-us-more-about-the-community-they-live-in-than-what-they-know-77934

Toh, T. L., & Yeo, J. B. W. (Eds.). (2019). Big ideas in mathematics. *Yearbook 2019.* Association of Mathematics Educators. https://doi.org/10.1142/11415

Tri-State Consortium. (2020). *Principles of responsible assessment.* http://www.tristateconsortium.org

Turkle, S. (2015). *Reclaiming conversation: The power of talk in a digital age.* Penguin Press.

Twain, M. (2010). *Letters from the Earth.* Greenbook. (Original work published 1909)

United Nations Educational, Scientific and Cultural Organization (UNESCO). (2013). *The global learning crisis: Why every child deserves a quality education.* https://unesdoc.unesco.org/ark:/48223/pf0000223826

U.S. National Commission on Excellence in Education. (1983). *A nation at risk: The imperative for educational reform.*

Valk, S. L., Bernhardt, B. C., Trautwein, F.-M., Böckler, A., Kanske, P., Guizard, N., Collins, D. L., & Singer, T. (2017, October 4). Structural plasticity of the social brain: Differential change after socio-affective and cognitive mental training. *Science Advances,* E1700489.

van Hover, S., & Hick, D. (2017). Social constructivism and student learning in social studies. In M. M. Manfra & C. M. Bolick (Eds.), *The Wiley handbook of social studies research.* Wiley.

Vico, G. (1710). *De antiquissima Italorum sapientia ex linguae latinae originibus eruenda libri tres* [On the Most Ancient Wisdom of the Italians Unearthed from the Origins of the Latin Language], translated by L. M. Palmer. Cornell University Press, 1988.

von Glasersfeld, E. (1990). An exposition of constructivism: Why some like it radical. In R. B. Davis, C. A. Maher, & N. Noddings (Eds.), *Monographs of the Journal for Research in Mathematics Education, 4,* 19–29. National Council of Teachers of Mathematics.

Vossoughi, S., Hooper, P., & Escudé, M. (2016, Summer). Making through the lens of culture and power: Toward transformative visions for educational equity. *Harvard Educational Review, 86*(2).

Vygotsky, L. S. (1962). *Thought and language.* MIT Press.

Vygotsky, L. S. (1978). *Mind in society.* Harvard University Press.

Wadsworth, B. J. (1989). *Piaget's theory of cognitive and affective development.* Longman.

Wagner, T. (2008, October). Expecting excellence: Rigor re-defined. *Educational Leadership* (Association for Supervision and Curriculum Development), *66*(2), 20–25.

Wagner, T., & Dintersmith, T. (2015). *Most likely to succeed: Preparing our kids for the innovation era.* Scribner.

Walker, L., & Warfa, A.-R.M. (2017). Process oriented guided inquiry learning (POGIL®) marginally affects student achievement measures but substantially increases the odds of passing a course. *PLOS One, 12*(10), e0186203. https://doi.org/10.1371/journal.pone.0186203

Watson, M. (2003). *Learning to trust*. Wiley.

Weingarten, R. (2020, April 8). This school year is far from lost. *Newsday, 80*(216), A27.

Zatorre, R. J., Fields, R. D., & Johansen-Berg, H. (2012). Plasticity in gray and white: Neuroimaging changes in brain structure during learning. *Nature Neuroscience*. Nature America. http://cogns.northwestern.edu/cbmg/plasticityInGM andWMreview2012.pdf

Zeiser, K., Rickles, J., & Huberman, M. (2016, August 31). Three studies show impact of deeper learning. *American Institutes for Research*. http://www.air.org /resource/three-studies-show-impact-deeper-learning

Zenner, C., Herrnleben-Kurz, S., & Walach, H. (2014, June). Mindfulness-based interventions in schools—A systematic review and meta-analysis. *Educational Psychology, 5*.

Zhao, Y. (2012). *World class learners: Educating creative and entrepreneurial students*. Corwin Press and NAESP.

Zhao, Y. (2018). *Reach for greatness: Personalizable education for all children*. Corwin Press.

Index

Page numbers followed by "*f*" indicate figures.

About the Authors

Martin Brooks is the executive director of the Tri-State Consortium, an alliance of over 50 public school districts in New York, New Jersey, and Connecticut. Previously, he was superintendent of schools on Long Island for 16 years. He also served as a deputy superintendent, elementary school principal, guidance counselor, and teacher.

Martin earned his doctoral degree in educational administration at Teachers College, Columbia University. He is a member of the Board of Directors of the Horace Mann League and has served on the boards of the Long Island Children's Museum, Public Schools for Tomorrow, the Metropolitan School Study Council, and the Long Island School Leadership Center. He is a member of the Suburban School Superintendents, the National Superintendents Roundtable, and the advisory committee for the Educational Leadership Department at Teachers College, Columbia University.

Martin has written extensively about education and leadership and has presented at numerous local, state, national, and international conferences. He is coauthor of *In Search of Understanding: The Case for Constructivist Classrooms* (1993, 1999). His current work involves helping school districts reflect on and improve instructional practice, curriculum, and assessment.

Jacqueline Grennon Brooks is professor emerita in the Department of Teaching, Literacy, and Leadership at Hofstra University, where she directed an institute that brought science to the general public and founded a clinical practice site for new teachers. Previously, she served as the founding director of a biotechnology teaching lab and a science discovery lab at Stony Brook University. At both universities she directed a secondary science education program. Jacqueline is a cofounder of the Long Island Explorium, a children's museum of science and engineering.

She is coauthor of *In Search of Understanding: The Case for Constructivist Classrooms* (1993, 1999) and author of *Schooling for Life: Reclaiming the Essence of Learning* (2002), *Big Science for Growing Minds: Constructivist Classrooms for Young Thinkers* (2011), and numerous chapters and articles.

Jacqueline holds an EdD in curriculum and teaching and an MA in developmental psychology from Teachers College, Columbia University, where she researched the development of constructivist teaching and infant–parent relationships, and an MS in urban and policy sciences and a BA in Education from Stony Brook University, where she learned just how complex policy and teaching really are.